ENGLISH
LEARNERS
IN
AMERICAN
CLASSROOMS

ALSO BY JAMES CRAWFORD

Bilingual Education:
History, Politics, Theory, and Practice

Language Loyalties:
A Source Book on the Official English Controversy

Hold Your Tongue:
Bilingualism and the Politics of "English Only"

At War with Diversity:
U.S. Language Policy in an Age of Anxiety

Educating English Learners:
Language Diversity in the Classroom

Advocating for English Learners:
Selected Essays

Diary of a Bilingual School
(with Sharon Adelman Reyes)

The Trouble with SIOP®
(with Sharon Adelman Reyes)

ALSO BY STEPHEN KRASHEN

Principles and Practice in Second Language Acquisition

Second Language Acquisition and Second Language Learning

Inquiries and Insights

The Input Hypothesis

On Course:
Bilingual Education's Success in California

Fundamentals of Language Education

Under Attack:
The Case Against Bilingual Education

Condemned without a Trial:
Bogus Arguments against Bilingual Education

Heritage Language Development

Explorations in Language Acquisition and Use:
The Taipei Lectures

The Power of Reading

Summer Reading:
Program and Evidence

English Learners
in American Classrooms
101 Questions, 101 Answers

UPDATED EDITION

*James Crawford &
Stephen Krashen*

DiversityLearningK12

PORTLAND, OREGON

For permission to reprint, send email to:
info@diversitylearningk12.com
Or send postal mail to:
DiversityLearningK12
P. O. Box 19790
Portland, OR 97280

ISBN 978-0-9847317-4-9

Library of Congress Catalog Number: LC3731 .C734

Library of Congress Subject Headings:
1. Education, bilingual—United States
2. Linguistic Minorities—Education—United States
3. Second language acquisition

Book design and typography by James Crawford
Printed in the United States of America
Updated edition, May 2015
10 9 8 7 6 5 4 3 2 1

CONTENTS

PUBLIC OPINION

INTRODUCTION

I T'S NO SECRET THAT IMMIGRANTS are transforming American classrooms. Or that increasing numbers of our students are ELLs—English language learners—a trend that poses unique challenges and opportunities for schools. How should educators respond?

Answering that question is the central aim of this book. While there are numerous excellent works on teaching ELLs, we saw the need for a basic but comprehensive introduction that would address the concerns of busy educators in a concise and accessible way. So we have strived to produce a state-of-the-art guide to our field, using a straightforward, Q&A format designed to focus sharply on the major issues.

For professionals seeking to do the best job they can for ELL students, several things are necessary.

First, it's essential to appreciate the dimensions of demographic and cultural change. The nation's Hispanic population has more than tripled since 1980, while its Asian and Pacific Islander population has quadrupled. Growth has been especially dramatic in Southern and Midwestern states where non-English-speaking groups were sparse until the 1990s.

Not only is the number of newcomers increasing; so is their diversity. Half a century ago, immigrants to the United States were most likely to arrive from Germany, Canada, Mexico, the United Kingdom, or Italy, in that order. Today, the top five source countries are Mexico, China, India, the Philippines, and Cuba. Other important nations of origin—each contributing 10,000 or more new Americans in 2012—include the Dominican Republic, Vietnam, Haiti, South Korea, Colombia, Jamaica, Iraq, Burma, El Salvador, Bangladesh, Pakistan, Ethiopia, Nigeria, Iran, Peru, Canada, the United Kingdom, Brazil, Nepal, Ghana, Guatemala, and Bhutan.[1]

---

[1] Rankings are for "persons obtaining legal permanent resident status" in the United States; refugees, asylum seekers, temporary workers, and other nonimmigrant admissions are counted separately.

On average, immigrants are younger than the U.S. population as a whole and are thus more likely to have school-age children. A large percentage of these children face language barriers in the classroom. Teaching them effectively requires educational approaches that are adapted to their needs and that seek to build on their strengths.

So educators' second major task is to master the pedagogies that work for ELL students and the scientific fundamentals behind them. This means learning about theories of second-language acquisition and their implications for educational practice, including the features and effectiveness of various program models.

To provide high-quality instruction for ELLs, teachers must be well-versed in this research. Among other things, they need to know about the difference between conversational and academic language; the importance of "comprehensible input" in English and the role of native-language instruction in making English input more comprehensible; how to use key methodologies such as sheltering and scaffolding; and the transfer of literacy between languages.

For administrators who make program decisions, it's also important to understand the debates about language of instruction. Should children be taught bilingually or in all-English classrooms? What are the options within each approach and how do they differ in methods and goals? What are the advantages and disadvantages for children? What do parents and communities want?

Our view is that bilingual education is usually a superior alternative for ELL students. A large body of research shows that, other things being equal, bilingual programs are more successful in teaching English and in fostering academic achievement in English. They can also provide valuable opportunities to cultivate bilingualism and biliteracy, not only for ELLs but for English-speaking students as well. Bear in mind, of course, that such programs vary widely in curriculum and pedagogical methods; so generalizations can be tricky. In addition, bilingual education is not always possible, for practical and sometimes for political reasons. But where it is feasible, it should be seriously considered, especially in teaching students with the greatest academic and language needs.

Third, educators must learn to cope with external pressures and become strong advocates for the programs that best serve ELLs. Perhaps no other area of education has been more politicized in recent years. Immigration has become a stormy controversy and language a frequent lightning rod. "English-only" activism—or a desire to avoid it—can complicate decision-making by school boards and superintendents. To resist such campaigns, it's necessary to learn how their arguments are frequently based on misconceptions and misinformation about language diversity.

At the same time, teachers feel increasing pressure from federal and state "accountability" systems that rely heavily on standardized test scores. ELLs rarely perform well on such tests, the vast majority of which are designed for native speakers of English. Yet under the No Child Left Behind Act of 2001, schools are threatened with punitive sanctions for "failure" if the ELL subgroup falls short of arbitrary targets for "adequate yearly progress." With the advent of the Common Core State Standards and the high-stakes tests attached to them, teachers' evaluations, salaries, and job security are now at risk. Students themselves are often denied promotion or graduation because of assessments that are neither valid nor reliable.

Thus it has become a challenge for educators to provide school programs that are based on pedagogical effectiveness rather than short-term expedience. They need to recognize the dangers of turning classrooms into test-prep factories, stressing remedial "skill-building" exercises, and narrowing the curriculum to two tested subjects, reading and math. To succeed in the long term, ELL students must have access to the kind of challenging education that all children need and deserve. It's our job as professionals to make sure that's what they receive.

This book is meant to be a starting point. Above all, we hope it will stimulate readers to learn more about this important and growing field.

STUDENTS

1 Who are English language learners?

ELL (English language learner) is the most popular term today for children who are sometimes described as *LEP* (limited-English-proficient[2]), *ESOL* (English for speakers of other languages) students, or more recently, *emergent bilinguals*. The meaning of these labels is roughly the same. All of them refer to students who face a formidable challenge: learning academic skills and knowledge while acquiring a second language at the same time.

This is a diverse population. A majority of ELLs are immigrants or the children of immigrants to the United States, with literally hundreds of national identities. Others are indigenous minorities, including Native Americans and Puerto Ricans. Although about three-quarters of these students are native speakers of Spanish, U.S. schools enroll ELLs from more than 400 language backgrounds. Substantial numbers speak Vietnamese, Hmong, Cantonese, Korean, Haitian Creole, Arabic, Tagalog, Russian, or Navajo. ELLs also vary significantly in socioeconomic status, cultural traditions, family literacy rates, prior schooling, English proficiency, and other factors.

If the past is any guide, the vast majority of these students will eventually become fluent speakers of English. Their problem is timing. By the time ELLs have acquired the language skills needed for school, their English-proficient classmates may have moved far ahead academically or, worse yet, their school years may have ended. To meet the needs of students whose English proficiency is limited, appropriate educational services are critical.

2 How is limited English proficiency defined?

There is no uniform definition at the national level. Each state and, in many cases, each school district set their own

[2] The term LEP has fallen out of favor because of its pejorative connotations (i.e., its focus on what students lack). ELL has become the preferred term among educators and will be used in this volume.

criteria for assessing and placing ELLs and for reclassifying them as English-proficient. A variety of tests are now in use for gauging progress in second-language acquisition. Such assessments are among multiple factors, including teacher judgments, class grades, achievement-test scores, and parental preferences, that are usually considered in deciding when children are ready to exit language-assistance programs.

Generally speaking, LEP or ELL students can be defined as those who come from language backgrounds other than English and whose difficulties in understanding, speaking, reading, and writing English are sufficient to create academic difficulties if they are placed in mainstream, English-language classrooms.

3 **What are the dimensions of the ELL population?**
ELLs represent about one in ten U.S. students today. Although immigration has slowed in the past decade, ELL enrollments continue to grow much faster than the overall school population. According to reports by states and school districts—the most reliable source of data in this area—there were 4.6 million ELLs in U.S. elementary and secondary schools in 2009–10.[3] Their enrollments increased by 25% in the past decade, more than four times the growth rate of the K–12 population as a whole (despite a slight decline beginning in 2007–08).

The largest numbers of these children attend school in California, Texas, Florida, New York, Illinois, North Carolina, and Arizona. Since 1999–2000, the fastest-growing ELL enrollments were in Indiana (274%), Mississippi (238%), Kentucky (228%), Arkansas (227%), North Carolina (188%), Alabama (185%), and Georgia (180%).

4 **What challenges do increasing numbers of ELLs pose for the public schools?**
There are several: designing effective programs, mobilizing adequate resources, finding appropriate materials, and dealing with

---

[3] This figure—4,647,016, to be exact—included ELLs in the 50 states and the District of Columbia; of these students, 76% were native Spanish speakers.

community concerns, among others. But unquestionably the biggest challenge for schools is to recruit and train sufficient numbers of qualified staff to serve ELLs' needs. This is true whether programs are bilingual or all-English.

Because this population has not only grown but also spread widely throughout the heartland, the number of U.S. teachers with ELLs in their classrooms multiplied from 364,485 (15%) in 1992 to 1,273,420 (43%) in 2002 (the latest figures available). Schools that rarely if ever served ELLs in the past are now scrambling to respond. It won't be easy. Only 11% of ELLs' teachers in 2002 were certified in bilingual education and 18% in English as a second language (ESL), while barely 15% were fluent in a language other than English. On average, these teachers had received just four hours of inservice training to serve ELLs over the previous five years.

5 What are the worst mistakes that schools make in serving ELL students?

Three common responses can be summed up as denial, delegating, and remediation. None of them is beneficial to ELLs.

Denial means ignoring the language barrier and offering students little or no special help in accessing the curriculum. Students simply receive the same instruction as English-proficient students. Sometimes described as *sink-or-swim,* this approach is destined to fail. It is also illegal under civil-rights law *(see Question 68);* nevertheless, it persists in some areas.

Delegating is what happens when administrators acknowledge there's a "problem" and turn it over to specialists—bilingual or ESL teachers—rather than involving the entire school in addressing the needs of these children. Sometimes a single, itinerant ESL specialist is given responsibility for students at several schools, a recipe for futility.

Remediation reflects an impulse to "cure" ELLs' "language disability" rather than recognizing—and, if possible, developing—the native language as a resource to support English acquisition. It also treats students as if they have a "learning problem," a none-too-subtle message that tends to be self-fulfilling. Remediation is increasingly a response to the pressures of high-stakes testing that stresses mastery of discrete skills in English. It often takes the form of *skill-building,* or the direct teaching of grammar and vocabulary, instead of more effective forms of ESL *(see Question 19).*

PROGRAMS

6 What types of instructional programs are designed to address the needs of ELLs?

Program models vary widely, even among those that share the same labels, such as "bilingual" or "ESL" or "immersion." Adding to the confusion is the fact that these models are not mutually exclusive. For example, bilingual education always features an ESL component and often uses immersion methods as well. With those caveats, ELL program types can be broadly characterized as follows.

Bilingual education is best defined as the use of students' native language to accelerate English-language development. Children receive content-area instruction in both languages, although the proportions may vary (with English phased in rapidly or gradually). Goals include developing "academic English," promoting academic achievement in English, and in some models, cultivating proficiency in both languages. Bilingual program types include the following:

- *Transitional bilingual education* uses the native language as a temporary support. Many transitional programs are *early-exit,* stressing a transfer to the mainstream as quickly as possible.
- *Developmental,* or *late-exit, bilingual education* emphasizes the goals of bilingualism and biliteracy—well-developed skills in English and in students' native language—as well as academic achievement.
- *Two-way bilingual,* or *dual language, education* is a form of developmental bilingual education that includes native-English speakers and limited-English speakers acquiring a second language and learning academic content in the same classroom.

All-English approaches make little or no use of students' first language. ELLs may receive some "native-language support," typically in the form of clarifications by teacher aides. But content-area lessons are in English only. Students may or may not receive direct instruction in English. All-English program types include the following:

- *Submersion,* a fancy term for providing ELLs no special help in overcoming the language barrier, was common before the Bilingual Education Act of 1968 and the *Lau v. Nichols* decision of 1974 *(see Question 68).*
- *Structured immersion* adjusts the level of English in an attempt to make content-area instruction accessible for ELLs until they have acquired enough English to survive in mainstream classrooms.
- *English as a second language* describes a range of strategies designed to teach English to students adjusting to an English-dominant society. ESL may be grammar-based, stressing a skill-building philosophy. Or it may be communication-based, emphasizing the use of English in meaningful contexts. Instruction may take place in a self-contained classroom or in "pull-out" sessions for individual or small-group tutoring.

7 What are the educational philosophies behind these different models?

All-English submersion and immersion models tend to reflect a *time-on-task* philosophy. The assumption is that the more exposure to English, the more English students will learn and the sooner they will be ready for the mainstream. Use of the native language is therefore seen as a distraction, or as a "crutch," that discourages students from using English. According to this logic, putting ELLs in a situation from which there is no escape will force them to acquire the language; hence the term *sink-or-swim.*

Bilingual approaches are based on a more scientific understanding of language acquisition. Rather than slow down or halt academic work while waiting for students to acquire English, bilingual models stress the importance of building on the linguistic foundation that ELLs already have.

The idea is that acquiring content-area knowledge in this way helps to make English instruction comprehensible and thereby fosters English acquisition *(see Question 9)*. In addition, developing literacy in the native language speeds up the development of literacy in English. Thus time spent learning in the native language is not wasted learning time. To the contrary, it is good for English as well as for academic achievement.

Bilingual approaches also draw a distinction between *conversational language,* a.k.a. "playground English," and *academic language,* the kind of English needed for success in school. This distinction has important implications for curriculum, instruction, and placement.

PEDAGOGY

8 Why does the conversational–academic language distinction matter?

Academic language refers to the decontextualized, cognitively challenging language used in school. Closely associated with literacy development, it is also essential in professional pursuits such as law, medicine, science, and journalism. In the classroom, academic language is required to understand story problems, write book reports, and read complex social studies texts. Indeed, it should be understood as a product of academic learning—not as a "higher" form of linguistic competence, but as a specialized set of skills that are essential for school success.[4]

---

[4] Various occupations and subcultures have their own specialized language, also known as *speech registers,* which must be mastered in order to participate successfully. For example, the language of boat-builders, farmers, or software developers can be as sophisticated as academic language, just different. Linguist Jeff MacSwan also notes: "There are numerous literate practices that are not normally taught in school, such as storytelling, text recital, rapping, songwriting, Morse Code, and Braille"; yet these nonacademic varieties of language often reflect high levels of linguistic competence.

Studies have shown that academic English takes considerably longer to acquire than conversational English, the kind of language that ELLs "pick up" through social interactions with English-speaking classmates and through beginning ESL classes. While conversational language is important, it is not sufficient for the purposes of school. Children who sound quite fluent in English in a relatively short time often do poorly when "transitioned" into mainstream programs. That's because they have acquired conversational English, but have yet to master enough academic English to enable them to understand instruction in regular classrooms.

Developing academic language—literacy in particular—requires instructional strategies that enable students to do challenging, grade-level work while they are acquiring English. This is quite difficult, especially for beginning ELLs, when instruction is in a language that students don't understand. All-English programs often rely on worksheets and other unchallenging material that are conveyed in simple language. This type of curriculum is boring and alienating for many students. It also fails to stimulate them in ways that engage them with school.

The good news is that bilingual education offers a solution. By using students' native language, teachers don't need to "dumb down" the curriculum. Well-designed bilingual programs teach grade-level material, helping ELLs keep pace with English-speaking peers while they are acquiring academic language.

9 How does native-language teaching help ELLs acquire English?

One might assume that the more English children hear and the more they are "immersed" in all-English instruction, the faster they will acquire the language. This turns out not to be true. Study after study has provided no evidence to support the time-on-task theory of language acquisition. ELLs who receive more native-language instruction in well-implemented bilingual programs typically learn more academic English than those in all-English programs (see Question 7).

Research shows that when we give children a good education in their native language, they get two things: knowledge and literacy. Knowledge and literacy, in turn, support English language development. The effect is indirect but powerful.

How does this work? What matters is the quality—not the quantity—of English exposure. The only English that helps is the English that the student understands. In other words, the more *comprehensible input* in English they receive, the more English they acquire. Knowledge learned in one language provides context that makes what children hear and read in a second language more meaningful. The positive effects of background knowledge on language acquisition (and on learning in general) have been thoroughly documented. The concept also makes common sense.

Consider the hypothetical case of a recently arrived ELL student enrolled in a high-school history class. While she has clear limitations in English, she has studied history extensively in her native language. She has learned a lot about World Wars I and II, is familiar with Louis XIV, Franklin D. Roosevelt, and Fidel Castro, and knows the locations of Istanbul, Addis Ababa, Copenhagen, and Bangkok. Thanks to the knowledge learned in her native language, she will have a context for understanding history taught in English. She is likely to make good progress in class, perhaps even better than that of some native speakers, and she will also acquire academic English.

10 Doesn't total immersion—being forced to "sink or swim" in a new language—make common sense, too?

Not really. When we can't understand a language, we don't acquire it. Incomprehensible input becomes undifferentiated noise, signifying nothing. It fails to "register" in the brain. What's more, being placed in a stressful situation that is demanding and unfamiliar only makes things worse. The anxiety and self-consciousness that result can interfere with our ability to receive input that might otherwise be comprehensible, a barrier known as the *affective filter*.

In other words, the sink-or-swim treatment actually retards the process of English acquisition, as well as academic achievement. Failure rates for children who were subjected to this approach (before it was outlawed) were extremely high. For those who survived, a common recollection is ... no recollection of anything that happened in the first two to three years of school—that is, until they began to acquire some English. Nothing comprehended, nothing learned. While a few ELLs were able to succeed despite the odds, it was often because they enjoyed advantages that their classmates did not *(see Question 37).*

11 But doesn't it help ELLs to practice speaking English as much as possible?

A common misconception—in laypersons' terms—is the idea that "practice makes perfect" in second-language acquisition. Also known as the *comprehensible-output hypothesis,* it assumes that we acquire language when we "produce" it, for example, in social interactions that prompt us to reformulate our speech so it becomes understandable to others.

This view confuses cause and effect. For ELLs, speaking English is the result of English acquisition, not the source. A phenomenon known as the *silent period* helps to illustrate why. Sometimes ELL students who have said nothing in their first weeks or even months of school suddenly start speaking English in complete, grammatical sentences. Their teachers are often shocked, having assumed that the students were making little or no progress in English. In fact, during the silent period they were acquiring the language through comprehensible input; no output was required. Now they are showing off what they have acquired.

In any case, ELLs simply do not produce enough language to account for the complex linguistic system they eventually acquire, and only a small percentage of what they produce is self-corrected (or corrected by others). Acquisition frequently occurs from listening and reading alone—that is, with no output whatsoever—which goes to show that "practicing their English" cannot be essential. Finally, it's important to note that there is no experimental evidence supporting the comprehensible-output hypothesis.

12 How does literacy development in the native language promote literacy development in English?

Literacy in the native language provides a shortcut to literacy in English. A simple three-step argument explains why:

1. We learn to read by reading, by making sense of what we see on the page.
2. If we learn to read by reading, it will be much easier to learn to read in a language we already understand.
3. Once you can read, you can read. Being literate in one language makes it much easier to develop reading ability in additional languages. In other words, *literacy transfers across languages.*

How do we know that transfer works? Several ways:

1. The process of reading is similar in different languages; readers of different languages use the same strategies to make sense of print.
2. Learning to read also happens in similar ways. In both English and Chinese, for example, vocabulary develops as readers pick up a bit of the meaning of a new word each time they see it in a meaningful context.
3. Studies show that students with more reading competence in their native language learn to read better in a second language.
4. Transfer has been documented even when writing systems are very dissimilar, such as from Vietnamese to English, Turkish to Dutch, and Arabic to French. In fact, whenever researchers have looked for evidence of transfer, they have found it.

The facilitating effect of native-language literacy may not be immediate. But it's clear that a person who is literate in any language will find learning to read easier in a second language than a person who is not literate.

13 Transfer sounds fine in theory, but does it really happen in the classroom?

It happens in every well-designed bilingual program. Here's an example:

Lorraine Ruíz taught a 2nd grade class of Spanish speakers in the Alum Rock School District in California. All of her students were ELLs. The children had exposure to oral comprehensible input in English, but much of the curriculum was in Spanish, and reading was taught exclusively in Spanish.

Ms. Ruíz had a classroom library with books in both English and Spanish. At the beginning of the year, the children could not read the English books, but by the end of the year they could. The children themselves were amazed. One child asked Mrs. Ruíz, "When did you teach us to read in English?" The explanation is that Ms. Ruíz helped them learn to read in Spanish. Once you can read, you can read.

14 Do ELLs need to be taught English phonics?

Phonics are the rules that enable us to read aloud merely by looking at letters, with no consideration of meaning. For example, we know that in English the letters *b-a-t* are pronounced *bæt,* regardless of whether we have any familiarity with baseball or with nocturnal creatures that fly around.

A common assumption is that phonics must be learned and taught "directly," so that students will have conscious knowledge of the rules. According to this view, we learn to read by applying these rules while we sound out or read aloud. A conflicting hypothesis is that our knowledge of phonics is *acquired,* or subconsciously absorbed, through reading. In other words, it regards phonics as the result of reading, not the cause.

Evidence from bilingual education lends support to the second hypothesis. Research has shown that knowledge of phonics gained in the native language is available for reading in the second language, provided that the writing systems are similar. Phonics in Spanish, whose pronunciation happens to be much more regular than that of English, seem to be all that most children need to acquire literacy in English.

It should be noted that teaching children the most straightforward rules, "basic phonics," can be useful. This is especially true for ELLs who have not learned to read in the native language. A conscious knowledge of some simple rules can help make texts more comprehensible. But drilling students in the complex and irregular rules of English phonics can be unproductive and even counterproductive.

15 How can phonics be counterproductive for ELLs?

Phonics are counterproductive when too many rules are explicitly taught and when these rules are overly complex. For example, the letters *h-o* at the beginning of an English word can be pronounced in nine different ways *(hot, hoot, hook, hour, honest, house, hope, honey, hoist)*. It is doubtful that any reader of this book consciously knows the rules for how *ho* is pronounced in each case. Nevertheless, we have acquired the necessary phonics, because we all know how to pronounce these words.[5] Many phonics rules are so complex that teachers report they have to review them before teaching them each year.

Not only does excessive phonics teaching cause needless frustration, but it also wastes time that could be used in much more productive activities. Some reading programs are so devoted to phonics that there is little or no time left for actual reading— especially of the free, voluntary variety that is especially important for ELLs *(see Question 38)*. In addition, it is likely that ELLs have not yet acquired the oral English that many phonics activities assume.

16 Are children in bilingual programs forbidden to read in English until they master reading in the native language?

Not at all. There is no reason to hold ELLs back in developing English literacy. The only criterion to consider is comprehensibility.

---

[5] Note that even if you knew the phonics rules for *ho,* you would not be able to read any of these words accurately left to right, letter by letter. To sound them out correctly, you have to look ahead.

Children can be encouraged to read in English as soon as they comprehend enough English to make the texts meaningful. Reading in the native language will make this happen sooner, because literacy transfers across languages and because the concepts that children learn through native-language reading will make English texts more comprehensible.

Many bilingual programs continue to stress native-language literacy even after children can read in English, because the benefits of transfer do not stop at a basic level. Throughout their school careers, children continue to develop academic language—a crucial component of *second-language instructional competence (SLIC)*.

17 What is second-language instructional competence?

SLIC refers to the level of language proficiency required to learn in English-language classrooms. It will vary according to the subject matter and the student's background knowledge. Young children are quicker to develop SLIC in mathematics than, say, social studies, because math is easier to contextualize using nonlinguistic means. By contrast, social studies involves abstract concepts that are hard to clarify with visuals and real-life objects; so SLIC takes longer to develop in that subject.

The weakness of many transitional, or early-exit, bilingual programs is that they transfer ELLs to regular classrooms before students have acquired enough SLIC to do well in an all-English environment. The urgency to "mainstream" ELLs often springs from a concern that children may "languish" in special programs without making academic progress *(see Question 48)*. Such worries are misplaced if children are enrolled in a well-designed bilingual program.

18 What are the components of a well-designed bilingual program?

There are three basic components:

1. Teaching content areas in the native language, without

translation. This builds subject-matter knowledge, which makes input in English more comprehensible.

2. Developing literacy in the native language, which transfers to the second language and provides a shortcut to English literacy.

3. Providing comprehensible input in English, first through ESL and later through "sheltered" instruction in academic subjects.

Developmental, also known as late-exit, bilingual programs provide a fourth component: development of the *heritage language,* or mother tongue of an ethnic community. These programs enable students to continue some classes in that language after they are no longer ELLs. The results—bilingualism and biliteracy—are beneficial not only to the individual student but also to society *(see Questions 28–30 and 101).*

19 How does ESL fit in?

ESL, or English as a second language, refers to special classes for ELLs, usually given for one to two sessions per day. Sometimes ESL is the only option provided for English learners, but it is always a part of bilingual education programs.

There are two fundamentally different approaches to ESL. The traditional *grammar-based* approach, sometimes called skill-building, assumes that we learn language when we are taught the rules of syntax and memorize vocabulary. According to this view, the rules are refined when our errors are corrected—requiring us to come up with better ones—so that grammatical correctness gradually becomes "automatic" through repetition. Over the last three decades, evidence has mounted that this is not the way language is acquired, either by children or by adults.

A newer, *communication-based ESL* approach begins with the idea that we acquire language when we comprehend what we hear or what we read. The result of receiving comprehensible input is not a conscious knowledge of language, but a subconscious "feel" for language, and the ability to understand and use it in meaningful contexts.[6] In this sense, language is *acquired* rather than *learned*. Effective ESL classes provide a natural setting that maximizes opportunities for acquisition to occur.

Depending on the approach, ESL programs have different goals. While the traditional goal is mastery of the grammatical system, the newer approach stresses the goal of using English for communication in ordinary conversation.

As important as this is, it's crucial to remember that conversational English goes only so far in the classroom, where academic English is needed for more complex, demanding purposes *(see Question 8)*. A more advanced ESL methodology, known as *sheltered subject-matter teaching,* as well as extensive meaningful reading, will stimulate academic language development.

20 What is sheltered subject-matter teaching?

Sheltered subject-matter teaching is a form of communication-based ESL instruction, in which the focus is on academic content—science, math, history, and so forth— taught in a way that is comprehensible for students with limited English. The goal in the minds of both the students and the teacher is mastering subject matter, not particular rules of grammar or vocabulary. In this way, students absorb academic English naturally and incidentally, while they are learning useful knowledge. If students are tested, they are tested on subject matter, not language.

Sheltered classes are appropriate for intermediate ELLs, who have acquired some conversational English competence. At first, subjects such as science or math are chosen because they can be more easily contextualized, that is, made comprehensible through the use of realia and pictures. Beginners in the second language are not included in sheltered classes, because the input will not be comprehensible for them. Fluent English speakers are not included either, because their interactions with the teacher and with each other may be incomprehensible to the other students.

---

[6] The study of grammar can be of some value to older students. Some of the "easier," more straightforward rules can be consciously learned and used for editing after students get their ideas on paper.

It's important to note, however, that not all programs that purport to provide sheltered instruction actually do so. A popular model known as *SIOP®* (Sheltered Instruction Observational Protocol) is advertised as "scientifically validated" not only for ELLs at all levels, but also for English-proficient students. In fact, SIOP's research claims don't stand up to close scrutiny. And its behaviorist pedagogy relies heavily on skill-building, while its prescriptiveness severely limits teachers' ability to be creative.

21 Does sheltered subject-matter teaching work?

Studies with intermediate, literate foreign-language students have consistently demonstrated the effectiveness of sheltered subject-matter teaching. Students in these classes acquire at least as much language as those in regular intermediate classes, and they learn impressive amounts of subject matter at the same time. Moreover, the kind of language they acquire is academic language, the linguistic toolkit needed for school success.

In bilingual programs, sheltered instruction can be used effectively as a bridge to regular, all-English programs. For example, an ELL student will learn math first in the native language, then in a sheltered class, and finally in the mainstream. This approach ensures that instruction is comprehensible at all times, while students are making the transition. No learning time is wasted.

Sheltering can be understood as a linguistic form of *scaffolding,* or a support structure to facilitate students' learning until they are able to progress independently. Just as sheltering helps to make a new language accessible, scaffolding helps to make the curriculum accessible.

22 Don't bilingual programs teach mostly in the native language?

Well-designed bilingual programs do not. Some critics have claimed that bilingual education requires children to spend five to seven years mastering their native language before they are taught English. This is untrue.

In a bilingual program, English can and should be introduced immediately. ESL begins on the first day, and subjects are taught in English as soon as they can be made comprehensible.

Research confirms that exposure to English is not delayed in these classrooms. According to one study of bilingual programs, by the time children reached the 3rd grade, 75% of their academic content instruction was in English; by the 5th grade, 90%. A study of late-exit programs, which feature a more gradual transition to the mainstream, revealed that 50% of instruction was in English by the 4th grade.

23 Why wait? Why not teach all subjects in English from the very first day?

Teaching only in English from day one does not speed up English acquisition. To the contrary, it slows students down. That's because all-English classes are not comprehensible for beginning ELLs, even if they are sheltered classes. It is virtually impossible to teach complex subject matter in a language that students do not yet understand. ELLs in such classrooms, receiving little or no comprehensible input, acquire little or no English.

A more efficient strategy is to give beginning students high-quality ESL to build English competence, along with high-quality subject-matter teaching in the native language. By introducing academic lessons in English after children have acquired some English and some content knowledge, instruction becomes much more comprehensible and progress is faster.

Let's say that you, as an adult, planned to study computers in Japan. But you know no Japanese and next to nothing about computers. You would benefit from a gradual transition as well. While acquiring some Japanese, it would make sense to learn something about computers in English at the same time. Plunging into computer science classes in Japanese right away would be a bad idea because virtually nothing would be comprehensible.

Now consider the experience of many ELLs, new to the United States, who are assigned to all-English classrooms with a little tutoring on the side, known as *ESL pullout*. It's no wonder that students in this situation make slow progress, both in English and in academics. There is no justification for treating children in this way when research shows there are better alternatives.

RESEARCH

24 Is bilingual education a better alternative?

Scientific evidence for the effectiveness of bilingual education is strong, abundant, and consistent. Research has repeatedly shown that well-designed and well-implemented bilingual programs are superior to all-English alternatives, both in teaching English and in promoting academic achievement. Nearly every scholar who has reviewed the *controlled studies* in this area has come to this conclusion.

Controlled studies are scientific experiments that are carefully designed to avoid bias from "background variables"—for example, differences in socioeconomic status or prior schooling between ELLs enrolled in a bilingual program versus ELLs enrolled in an all-English program. In this way, researchers can ensure a fair comparison of the educational alternatives. They know that if ELLs do better in one group, it's because the program worked better, and not because the students enjoyed special advantages that those in the comparison group lacked.

A rule of thumb in social science research is that results from a single study should not be taken as the last word. There is no "perfect experiment," especially when human variables are involved. On the other hand, considerable confidence can be placed in research results that are consistent from study to study, provided that researchers' methods are rigorous. Findings favoring bilingual education fall into this category.

Three major reviews of the scientific literature on ELL programs were completed in 2005. Although these reviews examined different studies for the most part, their conclusions were remarkably similar.

Not only did bilingual approaches prove to be more effective than all-English approaches, but they gave ELLs about the same "edge" in English reading scores. The advantage for bilingual education, while moderate, was nearly identical in all three reviews. This degree of consistency is rarely seen in educational research.

The latest *meta-analysis* of studies in this area, published in 2014, found that when both program quality and research quality are considered, the superiority of bilingual education was significantly larger than reported in previous analyses.

25 Are all bilingual program models equally effective?

No. Research findings have been more positive for developmental bilingual education than for transitional bilingual education. Two of the 2005 literature reviews only considered studies comparing any type of program using the native language for instruction versus any type of program using only English. The third review, however, also compared results between transitional and developmental bilingual education. It found a significantly higher "effect size," or advantage in academic outcomes, for developmental programs.

The results of a four-year longitudinal study sponsored by the U.S. Department of Education, released in 1991, are consistent with these findings: ELLs did considerably better in English reading and math when enrolled in programs that stressed bilingualism and biliteracy. Those enrolled in either transitional bilingual or all-English immersion programs did worse.

26 Are "dual language" programs the most effective?

Promising results have been reported for dual language, or two-way bilingual, programs, which have become increasingly popular in recent years. These models are designed to cultivate bilingualism among both English-proficient and limited-English-proficient students, taught side by side in the same classrooms. They often feature cooperative learning strategies, which have proven effective for both groups.

Two-way program models vary considerably in student

characteristics, community contexts, and the way the two languages are used for instruction. In some cases—for example, in bilingual communities—students may come from similar ethnic and socioeconomic backgrounds and have exposure to both languages outside of school. In other cases—such as in affluent areas where English is dominant—there may be stark differences in ethnicity and class that parallel differences in students' language backgrounds. These variations can have significant implications in the classroom and for the participation of parents.

Dual language instruction typically takes one of two forms. The *90/10 model* primarily uses the minority language (e.g., Spanish) for most instruction in kindergarten and 1st grade, phasing in English gradually until the two languages are used equally by 4th or 5th grade (a pattern also found in "one-way" developmental programs). The *50/50 model* strives to provide equal instructional time for both languages throughout elementary school, sometimes in response to parental concerns that English not be neglected. Each of these approaches has its enthusiasts, but so far neither has proven superior in all contexts.

Meanwhile, excitement about two-way models in general has inspired claims that they are the "most effective" form of bilingual education. There is good reason to believe that these programs can be quite successful in developing academic language. In addition, the benefits of bilingualism are undeniable for all children *(see Questions 28–30)*. A review of evaluation studies, however, shows there is not yet strong evidence that two-way programs are superior to other forms of developmental bilingual education for ELLs.

Also bear in mind that two-way programs currently serve only a tiny minority of English learners. Unfortunately, reliable statistics are unavailable at the national level.[7] In New York City, where a major expansion of dual language classrooms took place over the last decade, just 4% of the district's ELLs were enrolled in 2013–14.

---

[7] A directory of "two-way bilingual immersion" schools, started by the Center for Applied Linguistics in the 1980s, failed to keep pace with the growth of this model. Its criteria also excluded numerous programs mainly serving ethnic minorities.

27

Don't some studies show that immersion is better than bilingual education?

A few researchers say yes. But on closer inspection, the "immersion" success stories they cite are primarily foreign-language programs designed to teach French to English-speaking students in Canada. These are not alternatives to bilingual education. In fact, they are varieties of bilingual (and sometimes trilingual) education, which are designed to serve the language-acquisition needs of socially and economically "advantaged" members of Canada's majority ethnic group. French immersion programs have been very successful, but they have little to do with *structured immersion* for language-minority children in the United States *(see Question 6)*—programs whose value remains unsupported by research.

The contrast between Canadian-style French immersion and all-English structured immersion has been summed up as *additive* versus *subtractive bilingualism.* The first model, like developmental bilingual education, helps students acquire a new language while also supporting their native-language development. The second model essentially seeks to replace the native language with English. The difference between additive and subtractive bilingualism has major effects on minority children's cultural adjustment and on their academic and cognitive development.

28

What are the social implications of bilingualism for ELL students?

Immigrant children's adjustment, or *acculturation,* to a new society can take various paths. Some are quick to embrace English and American culture at the expense of their ethnic heritage, others become bilingual and bicultural, and a few remain largely dependent on their native language. Research has shown that each of these paths has implications for school performance, family relations, and life chances.

In the Children of Immigrants Longitudinal Study, a team of sociologists has been following the progress of 5,000 second-generation immigrants, primarily Latinos and Asian Americans, enrolled in U.S. middle and high schools. Among the study's findings:

- Students are making good progress in acquiring English; 94% know English "well," 64% "very well."
- Yet *language loss* is pervasive; only 44% know their community's heritage language "well," 16% "very well."
- A substantial majority of these students—72%—prefer to use English as their usual language.

The researchers reported that acquiring English alone was no guarantee of success in school or of psychosocial well-being. Children who had become largely monolingual in English rated lower in family solidarity and harmony, self-esteem, and educational aspirations than those who had maintained their bilingualism. Mastery of both languages, the study found, "helps anchor youthful identities by facilitating knowledge of parental cultures" while students are learning to function in American society. The overall conclusion: "While popular with the public at large, educational policies that promote complete linguistic assimilation contain hidden costs for these children, depriving them of a key social resource at a critical juncture in their lives."

Other studies confirm that second-generation children who fail to develop proficiency in the heritage language tend to experience serious communication problems with their parents and grandparents. Family relationships often suffer at a time when family support is critical to young immigrants' social adjustment and educational attainment.

29 What are the cognitive costs and benefits of bilingualism?

Many people still suspect that speaking more than one language is confusing to the brain. Indeed, that used to be the consensus among educational psychologists, based on IQ tests administered to immigrants in the early 20th century. Such studies turned out to be flawed because they failed to consider cultural, educational, and economic factors that biased the test results. Nevertheless, bilingualism was long viewed as a cognitive handicap.

Recent research points toward the opposite conclusion. Other things being equal, it seems that bilingualism may make us smarter. Bilinguals tend to outperform monolinguals on some tests of language and nonverbal intelligence, including the ability to think abstractly about language, or *metalinguistic awareness,* and one kind of creativity known as *divergent thinking.*

Other studies have shown that bilinguals are better at *executive control,* or ability to solve problems that require us to ignore irrelevant information and focus on what is important. They also have superior *working memories,* better able to keep information in mind while solving a problem. While both of these capacities decline in older people, bilinguals show less of a decline. In other words, bilingualism might reduce some of the negative effects of aging.

Fluent bilinguals also seem to do better in school. One study of Hispanic high-school seniors found that those who were proficient in Spanish slightly outperformed English monolinguals in English reading, and they expected to stay in school longer.

30 What are the practical advantages and disadvantages of bilingualism?

It's hard to think of disadvantages, unless one counts the ethnocentric biases (e.g., "This is America—speak English!") sometimes directed at those who speak other languages in public.

By contrast, the advantages of bilingualism are numerous. Beyond the obvious expansion of social and cultural horizons, speaking additional languages provides a competitive edge in business and the job market. A 1999 study found that in Miami, San Antonio, and Jersey City, Hispanics who were proficient in both Spanish and English earned up to $7,000 more annually than those who spoke only English. Similar patterns are evident in Quebec, where research shows that both Anglophone and Francophone bilinguals have a significant income advantage over their monolingual counterparts.

Just in the past decade, economic globalization has substantially increased the demand for bilingual proficiencies. While English has unquestionably become a global language, the preferred medium of finance and trade, it has hardly replaced the need for fluency in other languages. As the old adage goes, a business can buy in any language; to sell, it needs to speak the language of its customers.

Meanwhile, there is a critical need for diplomatic and military personnel who are knowledgeable in the languages of the Middle East and South Asia. The threat of international terrorism has created a booming job market for bilinguals with these skills.

31 How do former ELLs perform academically after "graduating" from bilingual programs?

Unfortunately, there are relatively few studies that track the progress of students after they exit bilingual classrooms. But the available research on this question confirms that children who complete bilingual programs and are reclassified as proficient in English do quite well in mainstream classrooms. One study reported that, on average, "graduates" of bilingual and ESL programs in San Francisco significantly outperformed native speakers of English in middle-school reading and math.

Of course, critics may argue that these are the "survivors," the gifted, or the otherwise exceptional few who prospered despite bilingual education. But the reports of such survivors are very consistent and include substantial numbers of children. They demonstrate, at a minimum, that bilingual education is not a pathway to failure.

32 How long does it take to acquire a second language?

Children vary significantly in oral language development. Some ELLs who start school as non-English speakers are able to carry on a conversation in English after a few months. Generally, they need more time—two to four years—to catch up with native speakers in conversational English. In one study, it took ELLs in elementary school an average of 3.3 years to achieve oral proficiency in the second language (although the range was considerable: from one year to 6.5 years).

Proficiency in academic English takes longer to acquire. ELLs usually need five to eight years, on average, to catch up to native speakers—in other words, to score at the 50th percentile level on tests of reading comprehension in English. This is a high standard, which by definition is never reached by 50% of native speakers. So the statement that "it takes five to eight years" to acquire academic English is oversimplified and misleading.

Also bear in mind that *English language proficiency (ELP)* assessments, required under the No Child Left Behind Act, remain a rather blunt instrument. As yet, they are unable to distinguish between the cognitive process of language acquisition on the one hand and academic learning, including literacy development, on the other. A student who scores less than proficient may be truly limited in English or may simply have reading difficulties. As a result, when these tests have been administered to other low-achieving subgroups, such as Native American students, they have "detected" many cases of limited English proficiency even among subjects who know no other language. Speaking a nonstandard dialect of English is another factor that may lower ELP scores.

The important question is how long it takes ELL students to reach second-language instructional competence, the level of English required to understand English instruction in particular subjects. Although no formal studies have investigated this question, it is clear that SLIC can be acquired in a much shorter time than is required to score at the 50th percentile or for *redesignation* as "fluent-English-proficient" (FEP).

Criteria for redesignation can be quite high, requiring academic language proficiency up to the 36th or even 40th percentile in some states. After five years, about 30% of ELLs meet such criteria. In the past decade, concern has been voiced about the many ELL students who are never reclassified, sometimes described as *long-term ELLs* (LTELLs).

33

Who are long-term ELLs and why are they performing poorly in English?

According to a 2010 study, 59% of California's ELLs in grades 6–12 had been classified as limited in English for at least seven years; by 2015, the figure had risen to 74%. A majority of these students were reportedly "stuck" at the intermediate level of English proficiency on the California English Language Development Test (CELDT), lacking the academic language needed to be redesignated as FEP. The recent attention focused on these so-called LTELLs prompted the state's legislature to pass a bill requiring schools to count and report the number of such students each year.

Several theories have been advanced to explain why LTELLs are faring poorly. Some are students with interrupted schooling because they have moved back and forth between the United States and their countries of origin. Others have been haphazardly assigned to various instructional programs from ESL to transitional bilingual education to mainstream classrooms. As a result, these students have been left with substantial gaps in reading and writing skills.

Another view of LTELLs is that they "have developed habits of non-engagement, learned passivity and invisibility in school, and have not developed the behaviors associated with academic success." The question is why. This analysis suggests that the problem is with the students themselves rather than with instructional programs that are failing to engage them.

Indeed, the term LTELL itself tends to reinforce that message. Conceptually, it conveys a *deficit hypothesis* that highlights children's "failure to learn English" after many years of schooling. The real problem may not involve language acquisition at all, but the type of schooling they have received. Seen as low achievers, such students often receive a steady diet of drills, worksheets, and memorization—a reliable recipe for academic alienation. Ironically, labeling them as LTELLs is likely to prompt calls for more remediation, rather than creative ways of motivating them academically.

A more promising solution would be for schools to do everything they can to encourage these students to read for pleasure. This is one of the major ways—perhaps *the* major way—of acquiring academic language. It's safe to say that there is no LTELL who is a dedicated pleasure reader in English and, in all likelihood, few successful former ELLs who are not.

34 Isn't it important to teach English early, since young children are best at language acquisition?

Starting early is always a good idea, since full proficiency in a language takes several years to acquire. But there is no reason for policies that push children into English subject-matter classes as rapidly as possible (which usually means before they are ready). Contrary to popular myth, older language students do as well as, or better than, younger students in language acquisition. So there is no danger, for example, that ELLs will be "left behind" if they remain in bilingual programs rather than making a quick transition to the mainstream.

Young children sometimes appear to be more adept acquiring a second language, for two reasons. First, they tend to be less self-conscious about making mistakes and thus speak more freely than adults. Second, they generally use the language in more social, less challenging contexts, making them appear more proficient than they really are. As a result of such impressions, ELLs are often mainstreamed prematurely, before they have acquired enough academic English to keep up in classrooms with native speakers.

Research has shown that ELLs who arrive later in U.S. elementary schools—after developing native-language literacy in their home countries—tend to acquire English faster and make better academic progress than ELLs who have been enrolled here since kindergarten. Despite less exposure to English, the late arrivals have a head start in academic language development, thanks to greater subject-matter knowledge and first-language literacy *(see Question 37)*.

In the 1960s, some linguists advanced a *critical period hypothesis,* arguing that our ability to acquire language declines sharply after puberty. Though consistent with folk wisdom, the idea that human biology plays this role has limited empirical support— especially when it comes to acquiring a *second* language. Recent research suggests that the capacity to master a new language starts to decline in early adulthood and may continue to decline with age. But the trend is gradual, not dramatic, and many who start acquiring second languages as adults do very well.

Moreover, the presence of a critical period—to the extent it may or may not exist—should not discourage the use of bilingual education. Well-designed, well-implemented programs do not delay English. To the contrary, they expose ELLs to comprehensible English, the only kind that counts, as soon as possible.

35 Do some children fail to develop proficiency in any language?

Except in cases of developmental disability, all children come equipped with a fully functioning *language acquisition device*. The ability to acquire language is as much a part of the human endowment as the ability to develop normal vision, hearing, hand-eye coordination, balance, and so forth. This principle applies equally in the case of deaf children, who acquire sign language—if given the opportunity—in much the same way that hearing children acquire speech.

The term *semilingualism* has sometimes been applied to ELLs and other children from poor and minority backgrounds, attributing their academic failure to a lack of proficiency in any language. Such judgments have been encouraged by assessment practices in some states, which require schools to test language-minority students' development in their native language as well as in English. In certain districts, substantial numbers of students have been classified as "non-nons"—that is, "nonverbal in both English and their native language."

This theory has been widely criticized on both scientific and pedagogical grounds. It has led to the misidentification of children as limited in their native language, either because they speak a nonstandard dialect or because assessments are actually testing academic skills like literacy rather than language development. As a result, many ELLs have been erroneously placed in special education or, at best, treated as slow learners.

Like earlier theories of "cultural deprivation," semilingualism is another example of a deficit hypothesis. It has functioned as a way of blaming students for failing to progress in school rather than analyzing how schools are failing the students. Not surprisingly, the ELLs who are mislabeled tend to be those with the lowest *socioeconomic status (SES)* and the greatest educational needs.

36   What impact does social class have on language acquisition?

There is no question that SES is a strong predictor of school performance. Numerous studies have shown a close correlation between household income and achievement-test scores for all students, including ELLs.

Social class differences are also associated with differences in rates of second-language acquisition. Higher SES means faster development of English, regardless of the measure used and regardless of whether bilingual education is available. Poverty has the opposite effects. In one study, 75% of children in the highest-SES group were reclassified as English-proficient by 5th grade, as compared with only 40% of the lowest-SES group.

Why does family wealth provide a significant edge? Higher SES brings obvious advantages that have a major effect on school performance, such as better nutrition and health care, fewer social problems, and less family mobility in search of employment or housing. Immigrant children from higher-SES backgrounds have typically had superior education in the native language before arriving in the United States. Even for those who came earlier, or were born here, there are profound benefits, including educated caregivers, tutoring in the native language, and more access to print, both at home and in better libraries.

Good schooling can compensate for some of these socioeconomic differences. Factors such as literacy development and academic support in the native language—characteristics of well-designed bilingual programs—can improve the achievement of low-SES students.

37

Why do some ELLs do well in school without bilingual education?

A common argument against bilingual education is that some ELLs have succeeded in all-English programs, gotten good jobs, and "made it" in America. A few have even gone on to become prominent politicians here. On closer inspection, however, many of these "success without bilingual education" stories reveal advantages that most ELLs do not enjoy.

One "English-only" advocate, who arrived from Mexico at age 9 speaking no English, claims that he did very well in a sink-or-swim classroom. Soon, he says, he was "one of the top students" in the 3rd grade. But this student had been in the 5th grade in Mexico in a good school system. Besides knowing subject matter at grade level, he was fully literate in Spanish—just as if he had been in a bilingual classroom. This preparation would have made the English he heard more comprehensible and his literacy transferable to English. No wonder he did better than the average ELL student. He had experienced *de facto bilingual education*.

Another interesting "exception" is former California Governor Arnold Schwarzenegger, who claimed that he acquired English via "immersion." He recommended that immigrants to the United States do likewise and avoid the use of their first language.[8] Close examination of his case, however, reveals that the Governor was another beneficiary of de facto bilingual education: good schooling in German in his native Austria, which gave him subject-matter knowledge and literacy, and plenty of comprehensible input in English, including reading.

Such cases are quite different from those of children in poverty, who tend to lack an adequate education or well-developed literacy in their native language, have limited access to books, and live in communities where non-English languages are dominant. These are the ELLs who can benefit most from bilingual instruction.

---

[8] In 2005, Schwarzenegger went so far as to veto legislation authorizing native-language assessments for ELLs in California public schools, even though they were specifically allowed under the No Child Left Behind Act *(see Question 71)*.

38

Why is access to print so important?

Possibly the most powerful way of increasing the English competence of ELLs is *free voluntary reading.* This means that students select reading materials for themselves, with no requirements, no book reports, no need to finish each book they start—no "accountability" of any kind. Studies have repeatedly confirmed the ability of free voluntary reading to improve reading comprehension, vocabulary, writing style, spelling, and grammatical competence among children, teenagers, and adults. The results apply to first- and second-language development in different countries and in a wide range of situations.

Reading can also be encouraged by read-alouds, discussion of good books, teachers reading while students are reading *(modeling),* and scheduled reading times *(sustained silent reading)* during the school day. We also know that the reading habit "transfers" from the native language; ELLs who start out as pleasure readers in their first language tend to become pleasure readers in English.

There is no evidence that giving students rewards or other external incentives for reading has any long-term effect on students' reading ability or on how much they read. What is clear, however, is that they need plenty of comprehensible and interesting reading materials. Given access, most children read. This means that well-stocked libraries are crucial, especially for children with little access to books at home. ELLs often live in high-poverty neighborhoods with few bookstores or good public libraries.

HERITAGE LANGUAGES

39

How effective is bilingual education in helping children acquire or maintain their heritage language?

Developmental bilingual models, both "one-way" and "two-way," can be quite effective. By enabling students to take academic subjects and acquire advanced literacy in the heritage language, they often lead to proficient bilingualism and biliteracy. Such programs have grown in popularity not only among immigrants but also in Native American communities, where language loss is widely perceived as a serious problem. For example, bilingual programs created to serve Navajo- or Hualapai-speaking children in the 1970s have been converted into programs to teach Navajo or Hualapai to English-dominant students.

Unfortunately, most developmental bilingual programs—including those labeled "late exit"—end by the 6th grade. Few bilingual classes are available at the middle- and high-school levels, and these are typically transitional in nature, designed to keep students from falling behind in demanding subjects while they acquire English.

Secondary schools sometimes provide programs dedicated to heritage-language development, such as *Spanish for Spanish speakers,* as an alternative to traditional foreign-language instruction. In addition, some community and religious organizations sponsor private schools that can be effective in teaching ethnic languages and cultures. While programs are diverse, they share the goal of preventing or reversing language loss.

40 What are the causes of language loss for children and communities?

Language loss among individuals, like *language shift* at the community level, has multiple causes. Sociolinguists have found that, over time, minority-language speakers tend to adopt a dominant language that has more power and prestige than their own. Language shift is encouraged by factors such as integration into the wider society; geographic mobility, especially from rural to urban areas; economic and educational advancement; exposure to mass culture in the majority tongue; intermarriage with other ethnic groups; and increased identification with the nation, at the expense of identification with another country or tribal heritage.

Historically speaking, among immigrants to the United States, the shift to English has been relatively rapid, a phenomenon that one linguist has described as "Babel in reverse." The trend shows no signs of slowing down, contrary to claims by some English-only proponents *(see Questions 91 and 92)*. It also affects Native Americans, most of whose languages are not being transmitted to younger generations. As a result, these ancestral tongues and the cultural traditions they embody are in danger of dying out.

At the individual level, three important factors help to explain failure to reach high levels of competence in the heritage language. First and most obvious is a lack of comprehensible input in that language. Studies show that if parents speak the mother tongue at home, children are more likely to acquire it. But if children only hear the language from their parents, there are likely to be limits on how far they can progress.

Two psychological factors also create obstacles. These are *ethnic ambivalence,* a stage some children go through in which they are reluctant or ashamed to use the heritage language, and a phenomenon known as *language shyness.*

41 What is ethnic ambivalence?

Children's attitudes toward the heritage language tend to be quite positive in the elementary- and middle-school years, but this can change. Some minority-language speakers go through a stage in which their desire to integrate into the dominant culture is so strong that they become apathetic or hostile toward the cultural heritage of their parents. This stage is known as ethnic ambivalence or ethnic evasion. Typically, it occurs during later childhood and adolescence, and may extend into adulthood. Those who experience such identity conflicts not only have little interest in speaking the heritage language; they may even hide their proficiency.

42 What is language shyness?

Young immigrants or Native Americans who are less than fully proficient in their heritage language sometimes report that their efforts to speak it are met with correction and even ridicule by more competent speakers. Not surprisingly, these reactions make them self-conscious and tend to discourage them from using the heritage language. This, in turn, results in less input and less competence. It appears that heritage-language speakers tend to set very high standards for themselves, and for others.

One advantage of well-designed bilingual and heritage-language programs is that they avoid practices that can "raise the affective filter," or create psychological barriers to language acquisition.

CRITICISMS OF BILINGUAL EDUCATION

43 **What are the criticisms of bilingual education that led to the passage of English-only initiatives in California (1998), Arizona (2000), and Massachusetts (2002)?**

These ballot measures required most ELLs to be placed in "structured English immersion" programs for "a temporary transition period not normally intended to exceed one year." Native-language instruction was generally prohibited before children were redesignated as proficient in English, except in certain cases where "waivers" of the English-only rule were granted at parents' request.[9]

The group that sponsored the initiatives, known as English for the Children, claimed that bilingual education was a failure because ELLs were performing poorly in school, dropping out at alarming rates, and "languishing" for years in Spanish-only classrooms without acquiring English. It accused schools of improperly assigning children to bilingual classrooms and keeping them there despite the objections of their parents, because state subsidies provided a financial incentive to inflate ELL enrollments. Finally, it characterized supporters of bilingual education as ethnic separatists.

---

[9] Rules vary among the three states. In California, a court decision has given the parents of ELLs some leeway to choose bilingual education, although procedures are confusing and hurdles remain high in many districts. By contrast, interpretations of the Arizona and Massachusetts measures have severely limited parental choices.

As we shall see, none of these charges was supported by evidence. Nevertheless, they reinforced public misconceptions and stereotypes. All three initiatives passed by wide margins.

44 ELLs score much lower on standardized tests than other students. Doesn't this show that bilingual education has failed?

The vast majority of ELLs take standardized tests in English, a language they have yet to master. So it should surprise no one that their scores are considerably lower those of fluent English speakers, for whom these tests were designed. This is true whether students are receiving bilingual education or not, because all-English assessments do a poor job of measuring what they know. If ELLs did well on these assessments, it would probably mean they were no longer ELLs.

In short, such test results are meaningless in judging the effectiveness of educational programs. Using them to draw conclusions about bilingual education is like criticizing an intensive care ward as substandard because its patients are sicker than those in the general wards of the hospital. This type of faulty logic was encouraged by the No Child Left Behind Act, with its high-stakes use of testing and failure to recognize what is unique about ELLs (*see Questions 71–73*).

45 Shouldn't parents have the right to choose whether their children are placed in bilingual education?

They already do. Under federal and state laws, the parents of ELLs must be notified of program placements for their children, and they may veto assignments to bilingual or other language-assistance programs. No doubt there are cases in which parents' choices are poorly explained or even denied. Schools are imperfect institutions. Yet there is no evidence that large numbers of children are being kept in bilingual classrooms against the will of their parents.

A state official in California, who oversaw ELL program compliance in the decade before the English-only initiative passed there, reported that his office had not received a single complaint during that period from a parent unable to remove a child from bilingual education. There were, however, numerous complaints from parents unable to get their children enrolled in bilingual education.

46 What types of programs do the parents of ELLs favor for their children?

Opinion surveys in this area have produced contradictory results because questions are often phrased in a misleading, either/or format. That is, many pollsters have implied that bilingual education is an alternative, rather than a means, to teaching English. In a typical survey of this kind, conducted in 1998, 73% of immigrant parents agreed that "public schools should teach new immigrants English as quickly as possible" rather than teach "subjects in their native language," thereby (the pollster implies) slowing down their English acquisition. By contrast, another poll that same year reported that 68% of Spanish-speaking parents supported bilingual education, including 88% of those with children currently enrolled in bilingual classrooms.

One thing is clear. Studies show that significant majorities of immigrant parents support the principles underlying bilingual education when they are clearly explained. Most agree that learning subject matter in the native language helps to make instruction more comprehensible in English and that developing native-language literacy speeds up English-literacy development. These responses have been consistent across both Hispanic and Asian groups.

In addition, like other ethnic minorities before them, today's immigrants tend to place a high value on the heritage language and hope their children will maintain it. Some parents prefer to achieve this goal through private means, such as "Saturday schools." Others welcome the role that the public schools can play through developmental bilingual education. Research has also shown that, when ELLs are enrolled in programs that make significant use of the native language, parents are more likely to help with homework.

47

Does bilingual education lead to segregation by race or ethnicity?

Avoiding segregation—an obvious danger when children are separated for language instruction—has been a concern ever since the rebirth of bilingual education in the 1960s. If ELLs have limited contact with English-proficient peers, they are less likely to make good progress in English acquisition and more likely to feel stigmatized as slow learners, often a self-fulfilling prophecy.

Bilingual programs have addressed this problem effectively by ensuring that ELLs are mixed with other students during lunch, recess, and often in classes like music, art, and physical education. In gradual-exit models, students join the mainstream in a subject as soon as they have acquired second-language instructional competence in it.

There is little that educators can do about segregation, however, when an entire school is segregated by race and ethnicity. This pattern is especially common for Hispanic students, who are most likely to be concentrated in poor, urban, majority-minority schools. At the elementary level, nearly seven in ten ELLs attend schools where at least 25% of students are limited in English.

48

Do children "languish" in non-English classrooms for many years, never learning enough English to transfer to mainstream classrooms?

This simply does not happen in well-designed bilingual programs. While the proportions of English and native-language instruction vary, depending on program model and grade level, ESL instruction is provided from day one, along with some subject-matter instruction in English (e.g., beginning with non-language-dependent subjects like music, art, and physical education). Typically, the percentage of English increases until it predominates by the 3rd or 4th grade.

In 2001–02, according to a nationwide survey, about 29% of ELLs were receiving some form of subject-matter instruction in the native language. Almost half of these "bilingual" programs were taught in English more than 75% of the time.

The rate at which students are redesignated as fluent in English and exited from special programs differs among states and school districts (although the data in this area remain fragmentary and unreliable in most locations). Still, there is no evidence that children are "languishing." In 2000, only 14% of ELLs in New York City who had started school in kindergarten or 1st grade remained in bilingual education after six years. That same year, an estimated 7% of such children in the state of Texas remained in bilingual education after the 5th grade.

ELLs in California have lower redesignation rates than in many states, owing to stricter criteria. These include scoring at least "basic" on the English language arts assessment administered to all California students (29% of whom failed to reach that level in 2005–06). Yet many who remain ELLs have nevertheless made the transition from special programs. That year, 42% of ELL students in California had met criteria that enabled them to study in mainstream classrooms.

49 Is there a tendency for schools to delay redesignating ELLs as English-proficient in states where per capita subsidies are provided to serve these children?

Critics of bilingual education have frequently speculated about this possibility, but without mustering any evidence that it has actually occurred. It seems unlikely that school administrators would make program placement decisions in this way. Here's why:

By conservative estimates, it costs at least 40% more to educate an ELL student than an English-proficient student. The additional expenses go for items such as inservice training, administrative support, instructional materials, language assessments, and teacher aides. State categorical formulas rarely provide enough funding to cover all of these extra costs. So, if anything, there are negative financial incentives to providing special services for ELLs, not to mention political pressures to exit students rapidly to the mainstream.

Most educators would agree that financial considerations should never determine whether children are retained in bilingual or ESL classrooms—or whether they are pushed out. Considering what research has shown about the consequences of a premature transition to English, many believe it makes sense to err on the side of extra language assistance.

In any case, as long as ELLs are receiving excellent instruction, there is no reason to worry about keeping them "too long" in special programs. The former ELLs who outscored native-English speakers in San Francisco *(see Question 31)* had spent, on average, 4.6 years in bilingual education or ESL.

50 What are the cost differences among various options for educating ELLs?

Contrary to popular assumptions, bilingual education is generally no more expensive than all-English models like communication-based ESL. Some bilingual program types, such as two-way (a.k.a. dual language), tend to cost more because they require additional administrative support. But the most expensive option is an all-English approach, *ESL pullout,* which requires an extra complement of teachers with special skills. In one California study, an ESL pullout program cost about six times as much as a developmental bilingual program. It also happens to be among the least effective pedagogical models for ELLs *(see Question 23).*

51 How can schools teach bilingually when ELL students speak several different languages?

Sometimes it is impossible. A "critical mass" of ELLs from the same language group, which is necessary to organize a bilingual classroom, may be lacking at some or all grade levels. In addition, schools may be unable to recruit bilingual teachers who are proficient in the students' languages, especially those from Asia or Africa. For diverse schools, a program of communication-based ESL and sheltered subject-matter instruction, combined with native-language support by paraprofessionals, is often the best solution.

Nevertheless, language diversity in itself should not become an excuse to avoid using the native language. Some critics of bilingual education have argued that it's "unfair" to provide Spanish-English programs when there are ELLs who speak Vietnamese, Russian, or Somali in the same school.[10] But the principle of equal deprivation is not one that many educators would endorse. A range of program options, bilingual and otherwise, is more likely to serve the needs of children. Research suggests that ELLs with the lowest SES and the least exposure to English in the community—who are often Spanish speakers—are most likely to benefit from bilingual instruction (see Question 36).

52 Doesn't the shortage of qualified teachers make bilingual education impractical?

There are also shortages of math, science, and special education teachers in many areas. Yet no one has suggested that we abandon those fields as impractical to teach.

Staff shortages—of both teachers and administrators—are common not only in bilingual education but also in ESL (see Question 4). ELL programs, whatever the approach, require well-qualified teachers who are knowledgeable about second-language acquisition, cultural diversity, and best practices in the classroom, as well as social and policy issues affecting the education of ELLs. Unfortunately, most colleges of education and the legislators who fund professional development programs have been slow to adjust to changing demography.[11] As a result, the number of certified bilingual and ESL teachers has failed to keep pace with the growing demand.

In an increasing number of states, first-year teachers are almost certain to have ELLs in their classrooms. Yet many are poorly prepared to meet the needs of linguistically and culturally diverse students. It's no wonder that many ELL programs are less effective

[10] This is an odd argument, since these critics also claim that bilingual education is ineffective.
[11] E.g., federal funding for ELL teacher preparation dropped by more than 60% because of spending limits imposed by the No Child Left Behind Act.

than they need to be. But the answer is not to abandon pedagogical approaches that we know can be effective. Instead, policymakers must invest in the personnel needed to make them work.

53 If bilingual education works, why is the Hispanic dropout rate so high?

Simple answer: there is no causal relationship, because not all Hispanics are ELLs and not all ELLs receive bilingual education. For example, in 1998, when California voters approved an English-only school initiative, less than half of the state's Hispanic students in grades K–12 were classified as limited-English-proficient and only about 17% were enrolled in bilingual programs.

Everyone agrees that the Hispanic dropout rate is too high. Calculating what the rate is can be tricky, however. According to an analysis by the U.S. Department of Education, 18.3% of Latinos aged 16–24 in 2008 were not enrolled in school and had received neither a high-school diploma nor a GED. The comparable figures were 4.8% for non-Hispanic whites, 9.9% for African-Americans, and 4.4% for Asians and Pacific Islanders.

A large percentage of these Latino dropouts, however, were born outside the United States. Many were recent immigrants who had never been enrolled in U.S. schools—nor in bilingual education. For Hispanic students born in the 50 states and the District of Columbia, the *status dropout rate* in 2008 was 10.8%. Still a concern, but hardly the "crisis" that's often hyped in media accounts.[12]

Several studies suggest that students who have been taught in bilingual programs drop out at significantly lower rates than similar students who have not. Rather than a cause of school dropouts, bilingual education seems to be part of the cure.

54 Then why do Hispanic students drop out of school at higher rates?

In general, students drop out less if they come from wealthier families, live with both parents, have parents who monitor

[12] Even the overall rate of 18.3% represents a dramatic improvement over the comparable figure for Latino dropouts in 1988, which was 35.8%.

their homework, have lived in the United States longer, or inhabit a print-rich environment.

Some of these factors appear to be responsible for much, if not all, of the disparity in dropout rates among ethnic and racial groups. About 40% of Hispanic students live in poverty, as compared with just 15% of non-Hispanic white students. Only 68% of the former live with both parents, versus 81% of the latter. When researchers control for such factors, there is little or no difference in dropout rates between Hispanics and other groups.

It should come as no surprise that students who report lower levels of English competence, and thus experience greater difficulties in school, tend to drop out more. But speaking a language other than English in itself does not have this effect. A federal study reported no significant difference in dropout rates between Hispanic young adults who speak English at home and those who speak Spanish at home.

A recent factor that seems to be exacerbating the dropout problem is high-stakes testing, such as graduation and promotion exams required in an increasing number of states. Summarizing the results of several controlled studies, one team of researchers has concluded that such testing programs are clearly "linked to decreased rates of high school completion."

55 If bilingual education is such a good idea, why don't other countries provide it?

They do. Bilingual programs designed to help children acquire the local language are offered in Norway, the Netherlands, Belgium, Germany, France, Spain, Sweden, Denmark, and Australia, among others. In addition, several countries in the European Economic Community (EEC) provide instruction in languages spoken by indigenous minorities, such as Basque, Catalan, Irish, Welsh, and Frisian, as well as in heritage languages spoken by immigrants. No member of the EEC has passed or even considered anti–bilingual education laws equivalent to those in California, Arizona, and Massachusetts.

Research confirms that bilingual education programs in other countries are successful, echoing similar results in the United States. Studies show that children in these programs acquire the language of the country at least as well as children in "immersion" programs, and they often acquire it faster.

56 Are bilingual educators promoting a hidden agenda of ethnic separatism?

Nothing could be further from reality. Unfortunately, some critics have tried to exploit ethnic stereotypes—for example, labeling bilingual education a "Hispanic jobs program" or a separatist political cause—rather than advancing fact-based arguments.

It is true that several Latino advocacy organizations (as well as groups representing Asian Americans) have enthusiastically supported bilingual education. But they have done so in the name of equal educational opportunity, not separatism. Even leaders of La Raza Unida Party, a militant Chicano group in the 1970s, adopted a transitional bilingual program that stressed the importance of English, when they were elected to the school board in Crystal City, Texas.

Some English-only proponents have argued that bilingual education is unprecedented because public schools never taught in other languages in the past and that government programs always operated in English. These claims reflect an ignorance of American history *(see Questions 82–87)*. Other critics express nostalgia for a "Melting Pot" tradition that requires immigrants to abandon their linguistic and cultural traits in order to be considered fully American.

Political viewpoints of this kind should not be used to limit the pedagogical options for ELLs. It's only fair that bilingual education be judged on its merits: whether it is successful in fostering the goals of English proficiency, academic achievement in English, and—when possible—heritage-language development. All-English approaches should be subjected to similar standards of effectiveness.

57

What has been the impact of English-only instruction laws?

Proponents of the anti-bilingual initiatives in California, Arizona, and Massachusetts argued that a mandate for structured immersion—a program specifically designed to last one year or less—would speed up English acquisition for ELLs. But in all three states, this has proved to be a hollow promise.

- A five-year study, commissioned by the California legislature, found no evidence that all-English immersion programs had improved academic outcomes for ELLs in the state or narrowed the "achievement gap" with English-proficient students. In 2004–05, only 9% of ELLs were reclassified as fluent in English— a rate that had barely budged since the year before passage of the English-only law.
- Researchers at Arizona State University reported that 60% of ELLs in Arizona made "no gain" in English in 2003–04, while 7% actually lost ground; all were enrolled in structured immersion programs. Another study found that the academic achievement gap between ELLs and other students in the state was widening.
- In Massachusetts, more than half of ELLs were still limited in English after three years in structured English immersion classrooms.

58

But didn't ELLs' test scores go up in California after bilingual education was eliminated?

This question is based on a misconception. In fact, significant (though declining) numbers of California's ELL students have remained in bilingual education, thanks to a flexible interpretation of the law's parental choice provisions.[13]

It is true that ELLs' scores on the Stanford 9 test rose following the initiative's passage, as widely reported in national media. But so did

[13] According to the California Language Census, 71,809 of the state's ELLs (5%) were enrolled in full-fledged bilingual programs in 2010–11, down from 409,879 (29%) in 1997–98, the year before the English-only law took effect.

the scores of *all groups* in California—including students who were rich, poor, white, minority, in all-English classrooms, and in bilingual classrooms.

As it happened, the Stanford 9 test was introduced the year before the English-only law took effect. Scores increased each year thereafter, as teachers and students became more familiar with the test, an "inflationary" pattern that has been well documented elsewhere when new standardized tests are introduced. Researchers have found no differences among ELL scores in California districts that continued to provide bilingual education, those that had eliminated bilingual education, and those that had never offered bilingual education. In short, there is no evidence that imposing all-English programs can be credited for increased academic performance by these students.

59   What about the Oceanside school district, whose all-English programs have received so much favorable attention?

Given the variability of achievement-test results, it's easy to cherry-pick certain schools or certain districts to "prove" virtually any point. But such claims have nothing to do with scientific evidence.

Reports about student progress in the Oceanside school district, as widely circulated by the *New York Times* and other media, were part of an organized campaign to promote English-only initiatives in other states. Dramatic improvements were cited in ELLs' Stanford 9 scores two years after the district eliminated all bilingual education in favor of structured immersion in English. By 2000, scores had indeed risen—to around the statewide average for ELLs—from a very low "baseline" level in 1998.

One likely explanation was that, prior to passage of California's English-only law, Oceanside's bilingual program had been substandard. According to the district's superintendent, the program had provided little or no English instruction for ELLs' first four years or longer. Introducing English would obviously improve results on English-language tests.[14]

In any case, the "Oceanside miracle" ended abruptly in 2001; since then, scores for ELLs in Oceanside have declined, relative to statewide scores, at most grade levels. Meanwhile, districts that had continued to provide bilingual instruction, such as San Francisco, were receiving limited attention for ELL test scores considerably higher than those at Oceanside. What does this prove? Only the capricious habits of news media. To draw any reliable comparisons about the outcomes of ELL program models, controlled scientific studies are necessary. Such studies have repeatedly confirmed the effectiveness of bilingual education.

60 How can bilingual education be improved?

Simply using students' native language for instruction is no panacea for ELLs (any more than it is for English-proficient students). Numerous other factors are essential in developing effective programs. Indeed, a major goal of the federal Bilingual Education Act was to assist districts in *capacity-building* to improve schooling for ELLs.

One simple and cost-effective way to strengthen bilingual programs is to enrich the print environment *(see Question 38)*. The number of books per child in elementary-school libraries is a significant and strong predictor of reading scores. Yet print resources are severely limited in languages other than English. A study of school libraries in southern California found only one book per child in the native language spoken by ELLs, and these were in schools providing bilingual education.

Other well-documented ways to improve ELL programs include:

- Strengthening the inservice and preservice training of teachers in language acquisition, understanding diversity, and effective practices in the classroom.

---

[14] Another possible explanation is that Oceanside's redesignation rate fell to 4% that year, about half the statewide average. So higher-performing students remained classified as ELLs, elevating average scores for the group. The following year, when redesignation increased to 18%, average ELL scores fell.

- Ensuring that bilingual teachers are proficient in the native languages of their students.
- Making all school staff responsible for educating ELLs rather than delegating the job to bilingual or ESL programs that operate in isolation.
- Developing schoolwide language policies that treat students' diverse backgrounds with respect, whether or not their languages are used for classroom instruction.
- Stressing cooperative learning and other constructivist strategies that involve ELLs actively rather than treating them as passive receptors of academic knowledge.

61 What is constructivism and why is it beneficial for ELLs?

Constructivism is an educational philosophy that begins with the premise, as expressed by Beverly Falk: "Learning is something that a learner does, not something that is done to the learner." According to constructivist theory, we learn by encountering new experience, assimilating it into what we already know or believe, applying those concepts to the world around us, and continuing to revise them in light of experience.

For true learning—as opposed to rote memorization—to occur, students must be actively involved in the process. Thus constructivist educators create environments that encourage questioning, examining, discovering, and creating. In such classrooms, students help to direct their own learning rather than simply absorbing what some higher authority claims they need to know. While this may sound like "anything goes," teachers play an essential role in guiding their students in productive directions, fostering collaborative projects, and making new knowledge meaningful through methodologies such as scaffolding and sheltering.

ELLs, who face the challenge of learning in a language they are still acquiring, are especially in need of such support. At the same time, they must be actively engaged. Those who are taught in traditional, *transmission model* classrooms (often organized around high-stakes tests), tend to find school tedious and irrelevant. These are the ELLs most likely to "tune out," fall behind, and eventually drop out. Although research in this area is limited, constructivism promises far better outcomes.

PUBLIC OPINION

62 Why did the "English for the Children" initiatives pass?

The reason is obvious: most people thought they were voting for English. A *Los Angeles Times* poll asked supporters of California's anti-bilingual measure why they planned to vote yes. Among likely voters, 73% agreed with the statement: "If you live in America, you need to speak English." Only 10% cited a belief that bilingual education was "not effective."

The wording of poll questions, as well as the official ballot summaries, offered voters a false choice: bilingual education versus English. The one survey that explained the fine print of the California law (mandating an all-English program limited to one year, threatening lawsuits against teachers who used the native language, requiring bilingual programs to be dismantled no matter how successful they were) produced very different results. Only 15% of respondents said they would vote for such a measure.

Most voters, however, made their decision on the basis of ballot summaries and press accounts that were often misleading. Widely publicized opinion polls in California, which erroneously reported strong Hispanic support for the English-only initiative, may have also played a role. On election day, Hispanic voters rejected the measure by a 2-1 margin.

63 What approach for educating ELLs is favored by the American public?

Again, survey results are contradictory, depending on how the survey question is worded. Generally speaking, the public recognizes the need to do something special to help ELLs with the language barrier and, of course, the need for these children to be taught English effectively.

A 2003 Gallup Poll asked the simple question, "Do you favor or oppose school districts offering bilingual education for non-English-speaking students?" Fifty-eight percent of respondents were in favor, including 72% of Latinos and 73% of African-Americans.

These results contrasted sharply with those of a 1998 Gallup Poll. That year it offered a choice between immersion, defined as "teaching students all of their subjects in English while giving them *intensive training* in how to read and speak English," and bilingual education, defined as "teaching students core subjects in their native language while providing them *gradual training* in how to speak and read English" (emphasis added). Not surprisingly, 63% of respondents chose the former program, which placed a higher priority on second-language acquisition. Just 33% chose the latter, which de-emphasized it.

It's clear that support for bilingual education becomes stronger, the better its role in teaching English is understood. Surveys with language-minority parents have shown that, when the pedagogical principles are explained, respondents express strong agreement *(see Question 46)*.

64 What role does ethnocentrism play in public attitudes about bilingual education?

In some cases, negative attitudes toward bilingual education reflect negative attitudes toward immigrants or particular ethnic and racial groups and toward the programs that serve their children. Such reactions have been encouraged and exploited by proponents of English-only legislation *(see Question 90)*.

Overall, however, ethnocentrism appears to be a secondary factor. According to one major study, a combination of anti-immigrant attitudes and "inegalitarian values" explained only 26% of the opposition to bilingual education. Negative attitudes stem primarily from a pervasive ignorance about bilingual education—what it is, how it works, and how effective it can be, according to scientific research.

65

Why is the public so misinformed about bilingual programs?

To begin with, the idea of teaching in two languages is unfamiliar to many Americans. Those who came of age in the mid-20th century formed their worldviews during the least diverse period, linguistically speaking, in U.S. history *(see Question 78)*. So it's no surprise that many have been slow to acknowledge or adjust to the realities of demographic change.

In addition, the news media have done a poor job of explaining bilingual education, often opting to fan the flames of political controversy rather than illuminate the pedagogical issues. A study comparing media coverage with research-based views between 1984 and 1994 found a remarkable disparity. While 87% of the academic articles were favorable toward bilingual education, that was true of only 45% of the articles in newspapers and magazines. In addition, less than half of popular editorials on bilingual education made any reference to educational research.

A final factor is that bilingual education researchers and practitioners have paid limited attention to informing the public about their work. Arguably, this should not be their job. But when a program is controversial, advocacy can be vital to the program's survival. Educators and academics have been slow to recognize this reality and act upon it. As a result, there has been a growing divergence between scientific findings on the one hand and federal and state policies for ELLs on the other.

LEGAL REQUIREMENTS

66

Does the federal government mandate bilingual education?

No. For a time during the late 1970s, the U.S. Office for Civil Rights required school districts found to have neglected ELLs' needs to adopt bilingual education as part of an overall remedy for their civil-rights violations. That policy was dropped in 1981.

For more than 30 years, the Bilingual Education Act of 1968 authorized grants to support instructional programs for ELLs. Most of the funding was set aside for approaches that used the native language and, from 1994 to 2001, for those that actively cultivated bilingualism and biliteracy. But school districts were only affected by these requirements if they applied for federal support.

In 2002, the Bilingual Education Act was replaced by Title III of the No Child Left Behind (NCLB) Act and was formally renamed the English Proficiency Act. All references to *bilingual* or *bilingualism* were removed from the text of the law. NCLB explicitly declined to require, or even recommend, any particular instructional approach in serving ELLs. But its accountability system provided strong incentives for schools to drop bilingual education in favor of all-English instruction *(see Question 73).*

67 Do states require schools to provide any particular instructional program for ELLs?

Most do not. A few states, including Texas, Illinois, and New Jersey, enacted laws in the 1970s (which remain on the books) requiring bilingual education for ELL students under certain circumstances. Similar mandates in California, Arizona, and Massachusetts were repealed by ballot initiatives and replaced with mandates for "structured English immersion" *(see Question 43).* In other states, such as Arkansas, Oklahoma, and North Carolina, laws dating from the World War I era prohibit instruction in languages other than English for any student, but these bans have gone largely unenforced.

68 What are schools' legal obligations in serving ELLs?

Under Title VI of the Civil Rights Act of 1964, federally funded programs are prohibited from discriminating on the basis of "race, color, or national origin."[15] School districts assumed they could meet this legal obligation by providing ELLs the same, all-English education they provided to

---

[15] Anti-discrimination provisions on sex, age, and religion were passed separately.

other students. But in *Lau v. Nichols* (1974), a unanimous U.S. Supreme Court disagreed, ruling that:

> There is no equality of treatment merely by providing students with the same facilities, textbooks, teachers, and curriculum; for students who do not understand English are effectively foreclosed from any meaningful education.

The court determined that districts must take "affirmative steps" to overcome language barriers obstructing ELLs' access to the curriculum. In other words, to provide these students an equal opportunity, schools must offer them a different educational program.

Lau did not impose any particular pedagogical approach. It simply required that schools provide some form of language assistance that would be effective. San Francisco, the defendant school district in the case, ended up expanding bilingual education for its Chinese- and Spanish-speaking ELL students.

69 In practice, what must school districts do to meet their obligations?

A "good faith" effort to help children overcome language barriers is not enough. Nor can a district cite financial constraints as an excuse to avoid providing effective programs for ELLs. Federal law guarantees students a right to equal educational opportunity—in this case, a right of access to the same school curriculum provided to English-proficient students.

But without specifying a pedagogical approach, how can civil-rights authorities determine whether districts are complying with the law? To answer this question, a federal appeals court established a "three-prong" test:

1. Programs for ELLs must be based on an educational theory recognized as sound by experts.
2. Resources, personnel, and practices must be reasonably calculated to implement the program effectively.

3. Programs must be evaluated and, if necessary, restructured to ensure that language barriers are being overcome.

Created in a 1981 case, *Castañeda v. Pickard,* this test was soon adopted by the federal Office for Civil Rights and by similar agencies at the state level. It remains the primary tool for enforcing the requirements of *Lau v. Nichols.*[16]

70 Are schools responsible for educating undocumented immigrants?

Yes. Under *Plyler v. Doe,* a 1982 decision by the U.S. Supreme Court, public schools may not discriminate on the basis of immigration status. It struck down as unconstitutional a Texas statute that had authorized school districts to exclude students who had no proof of legal residency. "These children can neither affect their parents' conduct nor their own undocumented status," the court ruled.

> Public education has a pivotal role in maintaining the fabric of our society and in sustaining our political and cultural heritage; the deprivation of education takes an inestimable toll on the social, economic, intellectual, and psychological well-being of the individual and poses an obstacle to individual achievement.

In accordance with the ruling, school authorities in most states are forbidden to inquire about children's immigration status or to require their parents to provide birth certificates, Social Security numbers, or other evidence of legal residency. Because *Plyler* was decided by a 5-4 majority, however, it has been challenged on several occasions by state laws designed to encourage the Supreme Court to revisit the issue.

The *Plyler* decision does not apply to undocumented students after they graduate from high school and, as a result, most have difficulty continuing their education. The DREAM Act, a bill introduced in each Congress since 2003, would permit such students

---

[16] Those requirements were also "codified" into a 1974 law, the Equal Educational Opportunity Act.

to qualify for in-state tuition at public colleges and universities, as well as legalized immigration status. But the legislation has proved controversial and, at this writing, has yet to pass.

ASSESSMENT & ACCOUNTABILITY

71 Has the No Child Left Behind Act proved to be an effective way to "hold schools accountable" in meeting these obligations?

Not so far. One problem is that this law contradicts the spirit of *Lau v. Nichols*. That is, it fails to recognize the unique situation of ELLs, requiring them to meet the same targets for *adequate yearly progress (AYP)* and, in most cases, to take the same standardized tests as English-background students.

Although NCLB does allow schools to assess ELLs' academic progress in their native language, such assessments rarely exist in practice. Most that are available are not "aligned" with state standards and may bear little relation to what students have been taught.

So the law relies primarily on achievement tests designed for native-English speakers. These are neither *valid* nor *reliable* in measuring what ELLs know. When tested in a language they don't fully understand, students may do poorly because of their limited English or because they haven't learned the academic material. There is simply no way to tell. Yet, under NCLB, these invalid and unreliable scores are used to make high-stakes decisions about schools.[17]

72 Why not depend on "accommodations" to help ELLs cope with English-language assessments?

Giving students extra time to take the test, allowing them to use bilingual dictionaries, and reading test questions aloud

---

[17] NCLB was due to expire in 2007, but it has been extended by a divided Congress unable to agree on a new version of the Elementary and Secondary Education Act (ESEA). Whether or not the law is replaced, the pitfalls of high-stakes testing for ELLs seem likely to persist under the Common Core State Standards.

are among the techniques that have been used to make academic assessments in English more comprehensible. Some studies show that such accommodations can raise ELLs' scores. Yet there is no evidence that they make the tests valid or reliable. Moreover, they place heavy demands on school staff, whose ability to provide them effectively is often limited.

In principle, it's unlikely that accommodations alone could ever solve the assessment problem, given the wide variations among ELLs in levels of second-language instructional competence. How could bilingual dictionaries, for example, be equally appropriate for children who speak very little English and for those who are nearly ready for mainstream classrooms?

73 Even if English-language achievement tests are inadequate for ELLs, what's the harm in using them?

Invalid and unreliable tests are worse than useless. They are frustrating and humiliating for children who find them incomprehensible. They are demoralizing to teachers who know that they and their students are being judged unfairly. What's more, they generate misinformation. Using inaccurate data to make high-stakes decisions about schools is not only pointless but also potentially damaging to programs that are working well. Yet this is precisely what NCLB has mandated in the name of accountability.

If all students, or even one of eight subgroups including ELLs, fail to make "adequate yearly progress," as measured by a single test of language arts or math, their school will face labels, sanctions, and other corrective actions that escalate over time. Ultimately, these penalties may include transformation into a charter school, takeover by state officials or private companies, and replacement of school staff. High stakes indeed.

Educators recognize that their careers are at risk, and adapt accordingly. Teaching to the test is a common response. Since achievement tests are overwhelmingly in English, it's not hard to imagine the impact on native-language instruction. As schools seek ways to boost ELLs' scores, they are abandoning bilingual education—often over the protests of parents and communities. Since 2002–03, when NCLB took effect, bilingual enrollments fell by 49% in California and 74% in New York City.

74 Are you saying we should scrap testing altogether?
Certainly not. Only that tests should be used appropriately, to serve the purposes for which they were designed.

A broad consensus among psychometricians, including those who work for the test publishers themselves, holds that a single test should never be used to make high-stakes decisions—for example, to retain a child in grade, evaluate a teacher, or punish a school for students' "failure." The reason is simple: there is too much uncertainty about what standardized tests actually measure.

Even the best academic assessments, those that have been carefully field-tested and found to be valid and reliable, can sample only a tiny part of what students have learned. That's why—in evaluating a program, for example—it's necessary to consider *multiple measures*, such as classroom grades and projects, portfolios of student work, enrollment in honors classes, and rates of attendance, promotion, and school completion.

75 If not for high-stakes purposes, how should tests for ELLs be used?
Above all, tests should serve the cause of improving instruction. That is, they should generate meaningful data that will assist educators in better serving kids. For example:

- Assessments of second-language proficiency can be useful in identifying ELLs, placing them in appropriate classrooms, and gauging their progress in acquiring English.
- Tests of academic knowledge, especially those that are locally designed, can help teachers diagnose the strengths and weaknesses of individual students.
- Such assessments can also be helpful in assessing programs, or comparing program models, for effectiveness.

- Standardized tests such as the National Assessment of Educational Progress (NAEP) can track long-term trends and relative performance between groups of students.
- Data from various tests, provided they are valid and reliable, can be used along with other criteria for accountability purposes.

76   How should schools be held accountable in serving ELLs?

Meaningful accountability involves more than standardized test scores. Enforcement of the *Lau v. Nichols* decision has focused broadly on the question of whether school districts are providing equal opportunities for ELLs. That means considering "inputs" like qualified teachers and effective program designs, as well as educational "outputs."

These principles are embodied in the *Castañeda* test currently used to enforce civil-rights laws for ELLs *(see Question 69)*, which could be adapted as part of a locally designed and administered accountability system. While allowing for state and federal oversight, this approach to accountability would reflect the priorities of parents and communities rather than those of distant bureaucrats. It would also be flexible enough to ensure that excellent programs are encouraged and supported instead of dismantled for failing to meet arbitrary achievement targets.

POLITICS OF LANGUAGE

77   What makes bilingual education so politically controversial?

Clearly, there's more at stake in this debate than the best way to teach a second language. Bilingual education raises a host of larger questions, such as immigrant rights and responsibilities, the role of English in our society, and even what it means to be an American.

These issues received little or no debate in 1968, when Congress passed the Bilingual Education Act. The law was intended to address the educational needs of language-minority groups—primarily Mexican Americans, Puerto Ricans, and Native Americans—that were long-established in this country. Large waves of immigrants began to arrive a decade later.

Opposition first emerged in the late 1970s, but an organized attack on bilingual education did not begin until the mid-1980s, with the rise of the *English-only movement*. Although important questions of language policy were raised, the discussion soon became polarized and distorted by factual inaccuracies. As immigration levels rose, "bilingualism" generated increasingly emotional reactions.

78 Why do some Americans find language diversity threatening?

Many believe that bilingualism is an unnatural and unhealthy state of affairs for nations in general and for the United States in particular. This is the central argument of the campaign to declare English the "official language."

It's a parochial perspective, to be sure, but hardly surprising. Americans who came of age in the mid-20th century tended to form their social views at a time when immigration was at a low ebb, and so was language diversity. Many were unprepared for the sharp influx of newcomers, mostly from non-English-speaking countries, over the past three decades.

Here's one way to view this trend, using 1960 as a baseline, when our foreign-born population was just 5%. Today's demographics look abnormal by comparison.

U.S. Foreign-Born Population, 1960–2010

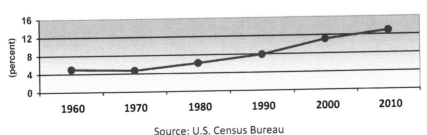

Source: U.S. Census Bureau

If we take a longer view, however, the perspective is quite different.

U.S. Foreign-Born Population, 1850–2010

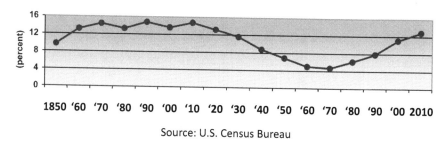

Source: U.S. Census Bureau

Notwithstanding its rapid growth in recent decades, the proportion of first-generation immigrants in 2010—12.9%—was barely above average for the past 150 years. It's safe to assume a similar pattern for minority-language speakers. The "abnormal" period was the mid-20th century, the least ethnically diverse in American history.

79 English is the official language in many countries. Why should this idea be controversial in the United States?

So far, no country has designated English as its *sole* official language, with legal restrictions on the use of other languages by government. Most nations where English is *an* official language— such as Canada, India, the Philippines, and South Africa—are officially bilingual or multilingual. That is, they grant legal protections for speakers of languages in addition to English. None has imposed the kind of *English-only* regime that today's official-English advocates are proposing for the United States.

It's true that some non-English-speaking countries have adopted repressive language policies aimed at restricting the expression of ethnic minorities. For example, Turkey and Slovakia have targeted the use of Kurdish and Hungarian, respectively, and have persecuted their speakers. Such draconian policies are inconsistent with American traditions of free speech and civil rights.

80

Isn't bilingualism a threat to national unity, dividing people along language lines?

Language diversity is a fact of life throughout the world, the normal state of affairs in all but a few small countries. This has been equally true in the United States, where hundreds of immigrant and indigenous tongues have coexisted with English. At least 381 different languages are spoken by U.S. residents today, according to the Census Bureau (school districts have counted even more; *see Question 1*).

As a marker of ethnic differences, language sometimes plays a role in ethnic conflicts. But diverse societies need not be divided societies. In a study of 130 nation-states, the sociolinguist Joshua Fishman found no correlation between linguistic diversity and civil strife. For every Canada, where language differences have become politicized, there is a Switzerland, where four language groups have coexisted harmoniously for centuries, enjoying equal rights under their constitution.

81

Why has language been a source of tension in Canada?

Canada is a good example of the polarization that can result from generations of social inequality based on language. Before 1969, French-speaking citizens had limited access to government outside the province of Quebec. De facto English-only policies made them second-class Canadians. Official bilingualism, adopted that year, was a belated attempt to guarantee minority rights. Unfortunately, it came too late to head off Québecois separatism in the 1970s, including French-only policies that have discriminated against English speakers.

The problem in Canada has not been language differences per se, but the use of language as a tool of ethnic domination. This phenomenon has been less common in the United States, where a libertarian tradition has largely prevailed and restrictive language laws have been the exception rather than the rule. As a result, Americans have tended to avoid major conflicts over language—until quite recently.

HISTORY

82 When has the official language issue come up previously in U.S. history?

Here are some key dates and events:

1923—First official-language legislation at the federal level, a bill to declare "American" the official language. This was a tongue-in-cheek assault on Americans who valued English literary traditions more than their own. It was not taken seriously by Congress. Nevertheless, the proposal was adopted that year in the state of Illinois, where Irish American legislators saw an opportunity to embarrass the British Empire. In 1969, Illinois quietly replaced "American" with English as its official tongue.

1981—First proposal to declare English the official language nationwide. Senator S. I. Hayakawa, a California Republican, introduced a constitutional amendment that provided: "Neither the United States nor any State shall make or enforce any law which requires the use of any language other than English. This article shall apply to laws, ordinances, regulations, orders, programs, and policies." The resolution never advanced in Congress.

1996—First Congressional vote on official English. By 259-169, the U.S. House of Representatives approved the English Language Empowerment Act, a measure designating English—and only English—as the language of most federal documents, communications, and services. The bill died in the Senate, which declined to act on it.

2006—First Senate vote on official English. An amendment sponsored by Senator James Inhofe, an Oklahoma Republican, would have declared English the "national language" and restricted access to government in other languages. It passed the U.S. Senate, 63-34, but died when the 109th Congress failed to agree on an immigration-reform bill.

WOW!

83

If the United States never declared an official language in the past, didn't this reflect the fact that—until recently—most Americans spoke English and nobody demanded government services in other languages?

Not at all. The United States has been linguistically diverse since before it became the United States. During the Colonial period, immigrants arrived speaking most if not all European languages; African slaves brought many others. In 1664, when the colony of New Netherland passed from Dutch to English control—and became New York—18 different languages were spoken on the island of Manhattan, not counting the numerous Native American languages spoken nearby.

To accommodate significant language-minority groups and solicit their support for the American Revolution, the Continental Congress translated important documents into German and French. German settlers were especially numerous. In the 1790 census, they represented 8.6% of the population of the original 13 states; millions more arrived as immigrants during the 19th century. German Americans established rural "language islands" *(Sprachinseln)* in states such as Pennsylvania, Missouri, Ohio, Illinois, Michigan, and Wisconsin, where their language thrived for up to five generations.

84

What did our nation's founders think about the role of English?

All of the founders saw the dominance of English as an advantage for the new nation, but most disapproved of language legislation. One exception was John Adams, who in 1780 proposed an "American Academy for refining, improving, and ascertaining the English language," modeled on the French and Spanish academies. The plan went nowhere in the Continental Congress. There was a general consensus among early leaders that government, especially at the federal level, should play no role in regulating the people's speech.

Meanwhile, there was some loose talk about replacing English—the language of King George III—with German, French, Greek, or

Hebrew as America's national tongue. But Roger Sherman, a delegate to the Continental Congress from Connecticut, summed up the majority view: "It would be more convenient for us to keep the language as it was and *make the English speak Greek.*"

85 As a practical matter, wasn't English always the language of government in America?

Mostly but not exclusively. It is worth noting that in 1783, when Americans won independence from England, Spain remained a major colonial power, laying claim to about half of today's continental United States. Spanish was the language of government in the earliest European settlements, St. Augustine and Santa Fe, as well as in San Antonio, San Diego, San Francisco, and many areas in between.

In 1800, Napoleon reclaimed the Louisiana Territory for France, then sold it to the United States three years later. When Louisiana joined the Union in 1812, French speakers remained a majority there. Congress required the state to keep official records in English—but *not only in English.* Until after the Civil War, the legislature and courts operated bilingually. Some officials, such as Louisiana's second governor, Jacques Villeré (1816–1820), spoke only French.

Beginning in the 1830s, states including Ohio, Indiana, Illinois, Iowa, Wisconsin, and Missouri translated laws and governors' messages into German and sometimes other languages, such as Norwegian and Welsh. California's 1849 constitution required all statutes to be translated into Spanish. In 1857, Minnesota printed its new state constitution in English, German, Swedish, Norwegian, and French. In 1875, Texas did so in English, German, Spanish, and Czech. New Mexico's 1912 constitution specified a variety of language rights for Spanish speakers, including a provision for the training of bilingual teachers.

86 But isn't it true that large-scale language assistance programs such as bilingual education appeared only in the 1960s?

Not true. In 1839, Ohio became the first state to adopt a bilingual education law, requiring instruction in both German and English where parents petitioned for it. Louisiana passed the identical legislation in 1847, substituting French for German. By the turn of the 20th century, about a dozen states and territories had passed statutes authorizing bilingual schools. Such instruction was often provided elsewhere without state sanction.

Surveys conducted in 1900 reported that 600,000 children in U.S. elementary schools, public and parochial, were receiving part or all of their instruction in the German language. This represented about 4% of the nation's elementary-school enrollment—larger than the proportion of students (from all language groups) in bilingual classrooms today.[18]

87

Weren't earlier immigrants more eager to join the Melting Pot and assimilate, as compared with those arriving in recent years from Asia and Latin America?

This is a racial stereotype that is unsupported by factual evidence. The same unfair charge was made against the so-called "new immigrants"—Italians, Jews, Greeks, and Slavs—who arrived at the turn of the 20th century. In 1911, for example, a federal commission accused these groups of failing to learn English as rapidly as the "old immigrants"—Germans, Irish, and Scandinavians.

In fact, German Americans, from Colonial times until the early 20th century, were more aggressive and more successful in maintaining their language and culture than most other groups. Pursuit of *Deutschtum* (German "identity politics") was combined with loyalty to an American nation-state based on democratic and egalitarian values, not cultural conformity. These aspirations were quite similar to those of *multiculturalism* today.

By contrast, the Melting Pot, as popularized by a play that opened on Broadway in 1908, espoused the goal of eliminating ethnic identities: "America is God's Crucible ... where all the races of Europe are melting and re-forming!" Some immigrants were enthusiastic at

---

[18] Heinz Kloss, the historian who collected these surveys, argues that one million, or 7% of U.S. elementary students, would be a more accurate estimate.

the time, but others resented the paternalistic and coercive
"Americanization" efforts sponsored by government and industry. In
any case, ethnic differences survived. As the sociologists Nathan
Glazer and Daniel Patrick Moynihan reported in 1963, "the point
about the melting pot is that it did not happen."

It is fair to say, however, that German and other immigrant
languages would have remained viable longer if not for the
xenophobic restrictions adopted during and after World War I *(see
Question 89)*. Coercive and repressive policies succeeded in making
the country less diverse.

88 Are you saying that policies to restrict languages other than English are inspired by xenophobia?

Language-restrictionist policies are never just "about
language." Inevitably, they reflect attitudes toward *speakers* of the
languages targeted for restriction. Some sponsors of English-only
legislation may sincerely believe they are espousing a "tough love"
position that will benefit immigrants by forcing them to acquire
English. Yet they tend to dismiss the discriminatory potential and
the message of intolerance embodied in such laws. It's easy to be
cavalier about the rights of others, with or without racist intent.

Coercive assimilation efforts are aimed primarily at immigrants
today, but indigenous minorities have been targeted as well.
Beginning in the late 19th century, the U.S. government imposed
English-only school policies that required Native American students
to be punished when caught speaking their tribal tongues.[19] As the
Commissioner of Indian Affairs explained the rationale in 1887:

> Teaching an Indian youth in his own barbarous dialect is a positive
> detriment to him. The first step to be taken toward civilization, toward
> teaching the Indians the mischief and folly of continuing in their
> barbarous practices, is to teach them the English language.

In fact, this was the first step toward *cultural genocide*. Virtually

---

[19] In the Southwest, similar "speak English only" rules were commonly enforced for
Mexican American students before the civil-rights era.

all the languages of indigenous peoples in the United States are threatened with extinction today, at great social cost to their communities. It was to help mitigate this catastrophe that Congress passed the Native American Languages Acts of 1990 and 1992.

89 Did European immigrant groups ever face this kind of cultural repression?

Rarely, but it sometimes occurred. During World War I, paranoia against German Americans led to emergency bans on their language throughout the Midwest. Use of the German language was outlawed on the street, in church, on the telephone, and in private as well as public schools.

Even after the war, states continued to enact English-only school laws. These were aimed especially at German speakers, but they affected all immigrant groups. Arguments in favor of such measures, like those in favor of official English today, were couched in the rhetoric of national unity. The most extreme of these laws prohibited foreign-language instruction before the 8th grade, a restriction that was later ruled unconstitutional by the U.S. Supreme Court in *Meyer v. Nebraska (see Question 98).*

LANGUAGE POLICY

90 Why does a large percentage of the public favor making English the official language, according to opinion polls?

Ethnocentrism clearly plays a role, but lack of knowledge probably plays a bigger one. Frequently, on first hearing about the official-English issue, monolingual Americans fail to see the downside. Many wonder, since English is so dominant in this country, whether it isn't *already* the official language. And if not, why not? This reaction is not surprising since—compared with citizens of many other nations—Americans today have limited experience with the politics of language. But when the potential impact of official English is explained, support drops off sharply.

Favoring English as the official language, in itself, should not be equated with racism. Yet it's undeniable that English-only fervor has ebbed and flowed along with waves of anti-immigrant activism. Racist attitudes—toward Latinos and sometimes toward Asians—have been closely associated with this movement. U.S. English, the first and largest English-only group, was a spinoff from the immigration-restriction lobby. Its founder was forced to resign in 1988 after he wrote a memo containing vicious anti-Hispanic stereotypes. That same year an internal survey commissioned by U.S. English found that 42% of its members, when asked why they had joined the organization, agreed with the statement: "I wanted America to stand strong and not cave in to Hispanics who shouldn't be here."

91 Immigrant languages are spreading so rapidly these days. Doesn't this trend threaten the status of English as our common language?

Certainly, with immigration at higher rates than, say, during the 1950s, it is now more common to hear other languages spoken throughout much of this country. In the 2010 census, one in five U.S. residents reported speaking a language other than English at home—although not necessarily to the exclusion of English. Both the number and percentage of minority-language speakers are clearly on the rise, as ethnic and linguistic diversity return to their historic norms (see Question 78).

Yet English is in no way threatened in the United States. That's because rates of English acquisition among immigrants and their children are also on the rise. In other words, the trend toward speaking non-English languages is balanced by a counter-trend toward increasing bilingualism. Between 1980 and 2010, while the number of minority-language speakers more than doubled, so did the number of fluent bilinguals—those who reported speaking English "very well," according to the Census Bureau.

If anything, the census figures understate the number of second-generation youth who are losing their heritage language. Other studies have shown a strong tendency for immigrant children to prefer English and to adopt it as their usual language *(see Question 28).*

Trends in Home Language Use and English-Speaking Ability, 1980–2010

	1980	1990	2000	2010	Change since 1980
All speakers, age 5+	210,247,455	230,445,777	262,375,152	283,833,852	+35%
English only	187,187,415	198,600,798	215,423,557	226,738,479	+21%
Other language at home	23,060,040	31,844,979	46,951,595	57,095,373	+148%
Speaks English "very well"	12,879,004	17,862,477	25,631,188	32,390,619	+151%
... not "very well"	10,181,036	13,982,502	21,320,407	24,704,754	+143%

Source: U.S. Census Bureau

92

How does this pattern compare with rates of English acquisition in the past?

Demographic data from a variety of sources suggest that today's immigrants are acquiring English more rapidly than ever before. According to the 2010 census, 95% of U.S. residents speak English "well" or "very well," and only 1.5% speak no English at all.

Language Spoken at Home and English-Speaking Ability, 2010

All speakers, age 5+	283,833,852	100.0%
English only	226,738,479	79.9 %
Other language	57,095,373	20.1%
Speaks English "very well"	32,390,619	11.4%
..."well"	11,290,723	4.0%
..."not well"	9,083,228	3.2%
..."not at all"	4,330,803	1.5%

Source: U.S. Census Bureau

The 1890 census, by contrast, reported that the proportion of non-English speakers was 3.6%—more than twice as large—at a time when counting methods were primitive. Even higher percentages were recorded that year in cities with substantial immigrant populations, such as Milwaukee, Wisconsin (20%); Manchester, New Hampshire (17%); and Fall River, Massachusetts (14%).

Indeed, the data show that it's *languages other than English* that are threatened in the United States today. Demographic studies have reported that, without the replenishing effects of immigration, most if not all of these languages would gradually die out.

93 Would it speed up English acquisition if government eliminated bilingual assistance programs?

Some people assume that if non-English speakers can read Social Security pamphlets or take driver's tests in their native language, they will have no incentive to learn English. Bilingual assistance programs supposedly convey the false notion that it's OK to live in the United States as monolingual speakers of Spanish or Chinese. Or that they encourage immigrants to be lazy when it comes to language learning. In fact, no real evidence has ever been mustered to support such claims—only personal anecdotes and ethnic stereotypes.

Bilingual accommodations are rare in any case. A 1995 study by the Government Accountability Office, commissioned by a sponsor of official-English legislation, could locate only 265 out of 400,000 federal publications—less than 1/10 of one percent—that were printed in languages other than English.

94 Isn't it important to send a message to immigrants that they are expected to learn our language?

People who face language barriers every day—on the job, in the supermarket, at the hospital—understand better than anyone the importance of proficiency in English in America. They don't need English-only laws to impress upon them this reality. According to surveys by the Pew Hispanic Center, a substantial majority of Latinos agree that immigrants "have to speak English to say they are part of American society." Meanwhile, 92% say it is "very important" for immigrant children to be taught English—a higher percentage than non-Hispanic whites (87%) or African-Americans (83%).

For many adult immigrants, the biggest obstacle to learning English is the shortage of affordable ESL classes. The problem is simple: inadequate funding from state and federal governments. English-only laws do nothing whatsoever to address this shortage. Rather than offering practical help to newcomers in learning English, they erect unnecessary barriers for those who are trying to do so. Outlawing bilingual programs now offered by government— and ruling out additional services in the future—would be counter-productive both for English acquisition and the acculturation of immigrants.

95 How do programs in other languages promote English and acculturation?

Bilingual voting materials, for example, which are provided in about 500 jurisdictions, have proven to increase political participation by language-minority citizens. A high level of English literacy is needed—higher than what is required for naturalization— to understand complex ballot measures and election procedures. In addition, there are native-born language minorities, including Puerto Ricans and Native Americans, whose English is sometimes limited. Language assistance at the polls helps these citizens become informed voters and gives them a stake in our democracy.

Another benefit: the more comprehensible American society becomes for newcomers, the more comprehensible English will become and the more English they will acquire.

96 Does this mean the United States should move toward official bilingualism, as in Canada?

There's no need for that. What would make more sense is a systematic effort to address language barriers that limited-English speakers face in accessing essential services and exercising legal rights. Executive Order 13166, issued by President Clinton in

2000 and reaffirmed by President Bush in 2001, is a step in that direction. The policy is grounded in Title VI of the Civil Rights Act of 1964, which prohibits discrimination on the basis of national origin in federally supported activities. It requires U.S. government agencies—and, equally important, programs that receive federal funding—to develop plans and procedures to "provide meaningful access" for those whose English is limited. Unfortunately, compliance has been minimal thus far, in both Democratic and Republican administrations. English-only advocates in Congress have actively opposed the order.

97 Backers of official English have disclaimed the "English-only" label. Aren't they advocating something less extreme than that?

In fact, it was the U.S. English organization that invented the term back in 1984, when it sponsored a ballot initiative in California entitled "Voting Materials in English Only." The label stuck because it accurately sums up the official-English agenda: banning or restricting the use of other languages.

For example, a 1988 ballot initiative in Arizona mandated: *"This state shall act in English and no other language."* The measure was so extreme that it even applied to state legislators, who were forbidden to communicate with constituents in any language but English. It passed narrowly but was later ruled unconstitutional and never took effect.[20]

98 How does official-English legislation violate the constitution?

The Arizona measure was struck down because it infringed the First Amendment guarantee of *freedom of speech* and the Fourteenth Amendment guarantee of *equal protection* of the laws. The English-only law not only violated the rights of state employees and elected officials to express themselves, the Arizona

---

[20] In 2006, Arizona voters adopted a less restrictive version of official English, along with three initiatives designed to limit the rights of undocumented immigrants.

Supreme Court found. It also violated the rights of limited- and non-English-speaking persons to receive information "when multilingual access may be available and may be necessary to ensure fair and effective delivery of governmental services."

Government cannot abridge fundamental rights without a compelling reason to do so, and in this case the court found such a rationale to be absent: "The Amendment's goal to promote English as a common language does not require a general prohibition on non-English usage. English can be promoted without prohibiting the use of other languages by state and local governments."

In *Meyer v. Nebraska* (1923), the U.S. Supreme Court struck down an English-only law, which banned foreign-language instruction below the 8th grade. In doing so, it used similar reasoning to that of the Arizona Supreme Court in 1998. "The desire of the Legislature to foster a homogeneous people with American ideals prepared readily to understand current discussions of civic matters is easy to appreciate," the high court said.

> But the means adopted, we think, exceed the limitations upon the power of the state. ... [T]he individual has certain fundamental rights that must be respected. The protection of the Constitution extends to all, to those who speak other languages as well as to those born with English on the tongue. Perhaps it would be highly advantageous if all had ready understanding of our ordinary speech, but this cannot be coerced with methods which conflict with the Constitution—a desirable end cannot be promoted by prohibited means.

99 What is the legal impact of adopting English as the official language?

Naturally, the impact depends on the wording of the legislation, which varies considerably. Of the 27 active official-English laws at the state level, most consist of simple declarations: *"English is the official language of the state of _____."* These have had few, if any, direct legal effects.

Other versions, such as the English Language Unity Act, a bill introduced in the 114th Congress, would impose sweeping restrictions on the federal government's use of other languages. While allowing some exceptions for purposes such as national security, public safety, and foreign-language teaching, these measures would curtail most rights and services for non-English speakers, including the bilingual provisions of the Voting Rights Act. Among other things, restrictive official-English proposals would:

- ban most government publications in other languages, for example, to explain tax laws, veterans' benefits, medical precautions, consumer protection, fair housing rules, and business regulations;
- require naturalization ceremonies to be conducted in English only;
- prohibit the use of public funds to translate civil lawsuits or administrative hearings; and
- eliminate anti-discrimination guarantees for limited-English speakers in both public and private sectors, including the right of parents to receive school notices in a language they can understand.

100 Still, isn't there something to be said for the idea of uniting Americans through a common language?

Of all the arguments in favor of official English, this one is probably the most hypocritical. Ever since the campaign emerged in the early 1980s, its main effect has been to divide communities. Whenever this debate flares up, the news media report outbreaks of *language vigilantism,* as local officials and individuals take it on themselves to enforce discriminatory policies.

While many English speakers may not see a problem, the targets of English-only campaigns find them offensive and threatening. Opposing such legislation in his home state of Arizona, Senator John McCain asked: "Why we would want to pass some kind of initiative that a significant portion of our population considers an assault on their heritage?" This is a question that English-only proponents have never been able to answer.

101

With all the ferment over language today, doesn't government need to establish a comprehensive policy?

Yes. Strictly speaking, the United States has never had a language policy, consciously planned and national in scope. It has had language *policies*—ad hoc responses to immediate needs or political pressures—often contradictory and inadequate to cope with changing times.

Americans need a language policy that reflects our values of ethnic tolerance, respect for civil rights, and generosity in meeting social needs. Executive Order 13166 represents a modest advance *(see Question 96)*. But more explicit and enforceable guidelines are necessary to ensure that these programs are effective.

We also need a language policy that promotes language acquisition in ways that serve the national interest. It should begin by strengthening opportunities to acquire English, of course, but should not stop there. English alone is not enough in today's global economy. America needs *English Plus*—well-developed skills in many languages to enhance international competitiveness and national security—as a resolution introduced in recent Congresses makes clear.

Finally, we need a policy that values the languages of immigrants and indigenous minorities, recognizing them *not as a "problem" but as a resource.* Rather than attempting to stamp out language diversity with English-only laws, we should conserve and develop competence in multiple languages to encourage community harmony, foster cultural expression, and meet the nation's needs.

NOTES

Introduction

Hispanic population; Asian and Pacific Islander population:
Gibson, C.J., & Lennon, E. (1999). *Historical census statistics on the foreign-born population of the United States, 1850–1990.* Washington, DC: U.S. Census Bureau.

Humes, K.R., Jones, N.A. & Ramírez, R.R. (2011). *Overview of race and Hispanic origin: 2010.* Washington, DC: U.S. Census Bureau.

half a century ago; top five source countries:
Office of Immigration Statistics (2013). *2012 yearbook of immigration statistics.* Washington, DC: U.S. Department of Homeland Security.

1. Who are English language learners?

a diverse population:
Kindler, A.L. (2002). *Survey of the states' limited English proficient students and available educational programs and services: 2001–2002 summary report.* Washington, DC: National Clearinghouse for English Language Acquisition.

2. How is limited English proficiency defined?

no uniform definition:
Abedi, J. (2004). The No Child Left Behind Act and English language learners: Assessment and accountability issues. *Educational Researcher* 33(1): 4–44.

3. What are the dimensions of the ELL population?

one in 10 U.S. students; enrollments increased:
National Clearinghouse for English Language Acquisition (2002). *How many school-aged English language learners (ELLs) are there in the U.S?* Washington, DC: Author.

U.S. Department of Education (2013). *Biennial report to Congress on the implementation of the Title III state formula grant program: School years 2008–2010.* Washington, DC: Author.

4. What challenges do increasing numbers of ELLs pose for the public schools?

teachers with ELLs:
Zehler, A.M., Fleishman, H.L., Hopstock, P.J., Stephenson, T.G., Pendzik, M.L., & Sapru, S. (2003). *Descriptive study of services to LEP students and to LEP students with disabilities; Policy report: Summary of findings related to LEP and SpEd-LEP students.* Arlington, VA: Development Associates.

5. What are the worst mistakes that schools make in serving ELL students?
civil-rights law:
Lau v. Nichols (1974). 414 U.S. 56.

6. What types of instructional programs are designed to address the needs of ELLs?
program models vary:
Crawford, J. (2004). *Educating English learners: Language diversity in the classroom*, 5th Ed. Los Angeles: Bilingual Educational Services.

7. What are the educational philosophies behind these different models?
time-on-task:
Porter, R. (1990). *Forked tongue: The politics of bilingual education.* New York: Basic Books.

content-area knowledge, literacy in the native language:
Krashen, S. (1996). *Under attack: The case against bilingual education.* Culver City, CA: Language Education Associates.

conversational vs. academic language:
Cummins, J. (2000). *Language, power, and pedagogy: Bilingual children in the crossfire.* Clevedon, UK: Multilingual Matters.

8. Why does the conversational–academic language distinction matter?
numerous literate practices:
MacSwan, J. (2000). The threshold hypothesis, semilingualism, and other contributions to a deficit view of linguistic minorities. *Hispanic Journal of Behavioral Sciences* 22(1): 3–45.

longer to acquire:
Hakuta, K., Butler, Y.G., & Witt, D. (2000). *How long does it take English learners to attain proficiency?* Policy Report 2000-1. Santa Barbara: Linguistic Minority Research Institute.

Grissom, J. (2004). Reclassification of English learners. *Education Policy Analysis Archives* 12(36).

sound quite fluent:
Cummins, J. (1980). The entry and exit fallacy in bilingual education. *NABE Journal* 4(3): 25–29.

9. How does native-language teaching help ELLs acquire English?
more comprehensible input:
Krashen, S. (2003a). *Explorations in language acquisition and use: The Taipei lectures.* Portsmouth, NH: Heinemann.

positive effects:

García, G. (1991). Factors influencing the English reading test performance of Spanish-speaking Hispanic children. *Reading Research Quarterly* 26(4): 371–392.

10. Doesn't total immersion—being forced to "sink or swim" in a new language—make common sense, too?
affective filter:
Krashen, S. (1981). *Second language acquisition and second language learning.* New York: Prentice Hall.

failure rates:
U.S. Commission on Civil Rights (1971–72). Mexican American educational series. Report II, *The unfinished education.* Report III, *The excluded student.* Washington, DC: Government Printing Office.

11. But doesn't it help ELLs to practice speaking English as much as possible?
comprehensible output hypothesis:
Krashen, S. (1998). Comprehensible output? *System* 26: 175–182.

result of English acquisition; silent period:
Krashen (1981).

12. How does literacy development in the native language promote literacy development in English?
learn to read by reading:
Smith, F. (2003). *Understanding reading,* 6th Ed. Hillsdale, NJ: Lawrence Erlbaum.

Goodman, K. (1982). *Language, literacy, and learning.* London: Routledge & Kegan Paul.

literacy transfers:
Cummins, J., Swain, M., Nakajima, K., Handscombe, J., Green, D., & Tran, C. (1984). Linguistic interdependence among Japanese and Vietnamese immigrant students. In C. Rivera (Ed.), *Communicative competence approaches to language proficiency assessment: Research and application* (pp. 60–81). Clevedon, UK: Multilingual Matters.

Krashen, S. (2003b). Three roles for reading for language-minority students. In G. García (Ed.), *English learners: Reaching the highest level of English proficiency* (pp. 55–70). Newark, DE: International Reading Association.

13. Transfer sounds fine in theory, but does it really happen in the classroom?
an example:
Krashen (2003b).

14. Do ELLs need to be taught English phonics?
result of reading:
Smith (2003); Goodman (1982).

15. How can phonics be counterproductive for ELLs?
overly complex:
Smith (2003).

16. Are children in bilingual programs forbidden to read in English until they master reading in the native language?
no reason:
Cummins (2000).

17. What is second-language instructional competence?
level of language proficiency:
MacSwan, J. & Rolstad, K. (2003). Linguistic diversity, schooling, and social class: Rethinking our conception of language proficiency in language minority education. In C.B. Paulston & G.R. Tucker (Eds.), *Sociolinguistics: The essential readings.* Oxford: Blackwell.

18. What are the components of a well-designed bilingual program?
three basic components:
Krashen (1996).

19. How does ESL fit in?
not the way; acquired, not learned:
Krashen (2003a).

20. What is sheltered subject-matter teaching?
a form of communication-based ESL:
Krashen, S. (1991). Sheltered subject matter teaching. *Cross Currents* 18: 183–188. Rpt. in J. Oller (Ed.), *Methods that work: Ideas for literacy and language teachers* (pp. 143–148). Boston: Heinle & Heinle, 1993.

A popular model:
Crawford, J. & Reyes, S.A. (2015). *The trouble with SIOP®: How a behaviorist framework, flawed research, and clever marketing have come to define—and diminish—sheltered instruction for English language learners.* Portland, OR: Institute for Language & Education Policy.

Krashen, S. (2013). Does research support SIOP's claims? *International Journal of Foreign Language Teaching* 8(1): 11–24

21. Does sheltered subject-matter teaching work?
literate foreign-language students:
Krashen (1991).

Dupuy, B. (2000). Content-based instruction: Can it help ease the transition from beginning to advanced foreign language classes? *Foreign Language Annals* 33(2): 205–223.

22. Don't bilingual programs teach mostly in the native language?
exposure to English:
Mitchell, D., Destino, T. & Karan, R. (1997). *Evaluation of English language development programs in the Santa Ana Unified School District.* Riverside, CA: California Educational Research Cooperative, University of California, Riverside.

Ramírez, J.D., Yuen, S., Ramey, D. & Pasta, D. (1991). *Final report: Longitudinal study of structured English immersion strategy, early-exit, and late-exit bilingual education programs for language-minority students* (Vol. I). San Mateo, CA: Aguirre International.

Ramírez, J.D. (1992). Executive summary. *Bilingual Research Journal* 16(1/2): 1–62.

23. Why wait? Why not teach all subjects in English from the very first day?
more efficient strategy:
Krashen (1996).

24. Is bilingual education a better alternative?
scientific evidence:
Willig, A. (1985). A meta-analysis of some selected studies on the effectiveness of bilingual education. *Review of Educational Research* 55(3): 269–318.

Greene, J. (1997). A meta-analysis of the Rossell & Baker review of bilingual education research. *Bilingual Research Journal* 21(2/3): 103–122.

three major reviews:
Slavin, R. & Cheung, A. (2005). A synthesis of research on language of reading instruction for English language learners. *Review of Educational Research* 75(2): 247–284.

Rolstad, K., Mahoney, K. & Glass G. (2005). The big picture: A meta-analysis of program effectiveness research on English language learners. *Educational Policy* 19(4): 572–594.

Francis, D., Leseaux, N. & August, D. (2006). Language of instruction. In D. August & T. Shanahan (Eds.), *Developing literacy in second-language learners* (pp. 365–413). Mahwah, NJ: Lawrence Erlbaum.

latest meta-analysis:
McField, G. & McField, D. (2014). The consistent outcome of bilingual

education programs: A meta-analysis of meta-analyses. In G. McField (Ed.), *The miseducation of English learners: A tale of three states and lessons to be learned* (pp. 267–297). Charlotte, NC: Information Age Publishers.

25. Are all bilingual program models equally effective?

third review:
Rolstad, Mahoney & Glass (2005).

four-year longitudinal study:
Ramírez (1991, 1992).

26. Are "dual language" programs the most effective?

two-way bilingual programs:
Lindholm-Leary, K. (2001). *Dual language education.* Clevedon, UK: Multilingual Matters.

not yet strong evidence:
Krashen, S. (2005). The acquisition of English by children in two-way programs: What does the research say? *NABE Review of Research and Practice* 3: 1–20.

just 4%:
New York City Department of English Language Learners and Student Support (2014). *School year 2013–2014 demographic report.* New York: Author.

27. Don't some studies show that immersion is better than bilingual education?

a few researchers say yes:
Rossell, C. & Baker, K. (1996). The educational effectiveness of bilingual education. *Research in the Teaching of English* 30(1): 7–74.

French immersion programs:
Lambert, W. & Tucker, G.R. (1972). *The bilingual education of children: The St. Lambert experiment.* Rowley, MA: Newbury House.

Swain, M. & Lapkin, S. (1982). *Evaluating bilingual education: A Canadian case study.* Clevedon, UK: Multilingual Matters.

varieties of bilingual education:
Cummins (2000).

additive versus subtractive bilingualism:
Lambert, W. (1977). The effects of bilingualism on the individual: Cognitive and sociocultural considerations. In P. Hornby (Ed.), *Bilingualism: Psychological, social, and education implications* (pp. 15–27). New York: Academic Press.

28. What are the social implications of bilingualism for ELL students?

Children of Immigrants Longitudinal Study:
Portes, A. & Hao, L. (1998). E Pluribus Unum: Bilingualism and loss of language in the second generation. *Sociology of Language* 71: 269–294.

Portes, A. & Hao, L. (2002). The price of uniformity: Language, family, and personality adjustment in the immigrant second generation. *Ethnic and Racial Studies* 25: 889–912.

serious communication problems:
Wong Fillmore, L. (1991). When learning a second language means losing the first. *Early Childhood Research Quarterly* 6: 323–346.

Cho, G. (2001). The role of HL in social interactions and relationships: Reflections from a language minority group. *Bilingual Research Journal* 24(4): 369–384.

29. What are the cognitive costs and benefits of bilingualism?

turned out to be flawed:
Peal, E. & Lambert, W. (1962). The relation of bilingualism to intelligence. *Psychological Monographs* 76: 1–23.

Hakuta, K. (1986). *Mirror of language: The debate on bilingualism.* New York: Basic Books.

makes us smarter:
Cummins, J. (1976). The influence of bilingualism on cognitive growth: A synthesis of research findings and explanatory hypotheses. In C. Baker & N. Hornberger (Eds.), *An introductory reader to the writings of Jim Cummins* (pp. 26–55). Clevedon, UK: Multilingual Matters, 2001.

Hakuta, K. & Diaz, R. (1985). The relationship between degree of bilingualism and cognitive ability: A critical discussion and some new longitudinal data. In K.E. Nelson (Ed.), *Children's language* (Vol. V, pp. 319–344). Hillsdale, NJ: Lawrence Erlbaum.

executive control; working memories:
Bialystok, E., Craik, F., Klein, R & Viswanathan, M. (2004). Bilingualism, aging, and cognitive control: Evidence from the Simon task. *Psychology and Aging* 19(2): 290–303.

Bialystok, E., Craik, F. & Ryan, J. (2006). Executive control in a modified anti-saccade task: Effects of aging and bilingualism. *Journal of Experimental Psychology: Learning, Memory, and Cognition* 32(6): 1341–1354.

better in school:
Fernandez, R. & Nielsen, F. (1986). Bilingualism and Hispanic scholastic achievement: Some baseline results. *Social Science Research* 15:43–70.

30. What are the practical advantages and disadvantages of bilingualism?
1999 study:
Fradd, S. H. & Boswell, T.D. (1999). Income patterns of bilingual and English-only Hispanics in selected metropolitan areas. In S.H. Fradd (Ed.), *Creating Florida's multilingual global workforce: Educational policies and practices for students learning new languages.* Tallahassee: Florida Department of Education.

evident in Quebec:
Chorney, H. (1995). The economic benefits of linguistic duality and bilingualism: A political economy approach. In *Official languages and the economy: New Canadian perspectives; Papers presented at a colloquium.* Ottawa: Canadian Heritage.

old adage:
Simon, P. (1988). *The tongue-tied American.* New York: Continuum.

31. How do former ELLs perform academically after "graduating" from bilingual programs?
well in mainstream classes:
Burnham-Massey, L & Pina, M. (1990). Effects of bilingual instruction on English academic achievement of LEP students. *Reading Improvement* 27(2): 129–132.

Medina, M., Saldate, M. & Mishra, S. (1985). The sustaining effects of bilingual education: A follow-up study. *Journal of Instructional Psychology* 12(3): 132–139.

Curiel, H., Rosenthal, J. & Richek, P. (1986). Impacts of bilingual education on school grades, attendance, retentions, and drop-out. *Hispanic Journal of Behavioral Sciences* 8(4): 357–367.

significantly outperformed:
Ramírez, J.D. (1998). *Performance of redesignated fluent-English-proficient students.* San Francisco: San Francisco Unified School District.

32. How long does it take to acquire a second language?
two to four years:
Hakuta, Butler & Witt (2000).

3.3 years:
Pray, L.C. & MacSwan, J. (2002, Apr. 4). Different question, same answer: How long does it take for English learners to acquire proficiency? Paper presented at the annual meeting of the American Educational Research Association, New Orleans.

at the 50th percentile:
Collier, V. (1989). How long? A synthesis of research on academic achievement in second language. *TESOL Quarterly* 23: 509–531.

about 30% of ELLs:
Hakuta, Butler & Witt (2000).

33. Who are long-term ELLs and why are they performing poorly in English?
59% of California's ELLs:
Olsen, L. (2010). *Reparable harm: Fulfilling the unkept promise of educational opportunity for California's long term English learners.* Long Beach, CA: Californians Together.

risen to 74%:
Californians Together (2015, Jan. 5). Press release.

bill requiring schools to count:
AB-2193 (2012).

Various theories:
Menken, K. & Kleyn, T. (2009). The difficult road for long-term English learners. *Educational Leadership* 66 (7).

"habits of non-engagement":
Olsen (2010).

A more promising solution:
Krashen, S. and Williams, C. (2012). Is self-selected pleasure reading the cure for the long-term ELL syndrome? A case history. *NABE Perspectives* (Sep.–Dec.): 26.

34. Isn't it important to teach English early, since young children are best at language acquisition?
older language students:
Krashen, S., Long, M. & Scarcella, R. (1979). Age, rate, and eventual attainment in second language acquisition. *TESOL Quarterly* 12: 573–582.

mainstreamed prematurely:
Cummins, J. (1980). The entry and exit fallacy in bilingual education. *NABE Journal* 4(3): 25–29.

ELLs who arrive later:
Collier, V. (1987). Age and rate of acquisition of second language for academic purposes. *TESOL Quarterly* 21: 617–641.

"critical period" hypothesis:
Lenneberg, E. (1967). *Biological foundations of language.* New York: John Wiley & Sons.

limited empirical support:
Krashen, S. (1973). Lateralization, language learning, and the critical period. *Language Learning* 23: 63–74.

gradual decline:
Bialystok, E. & Hakuta, K. (1999). Confounded age: Linguistic and cognitive factors in age differences for second language acquisition. In D. Birdsong (Ed.), *Second language acquisition and the critical period hypothesis* (pp. 161–181). Mahwah, NJ: Lawrence Erlbaum.

35. Do some children fail to develop proficiency in any language?
Semilingualism; widely criticized:
MacSwan (2000).

36. What impact does social class have on language acquisition?
household income and achievement test scores:
Rothstein, R. (1998). *The way we Were? The myths and realities of America's student achievement.* New York: Century Foundation.

faster development:
Hakuta, Butler & Witt (2000).

obvious advantages:
Rothstein, R. (2004). *Class and schools: Using social, economic, and educational reform to close the black-white achievement gap.* Washington, DC: Economic Policy Institute.

higher SES backgrounds:
Tse, L. (2001). *Why don't they learn English? Separating fact from fallacy in the U.S. language debate.* New York: Teachers College Press.

37. Why do some ELLs do well in school without bilingual education?
"English-only" advocate:
de la Peña, F. (1991). *Democracy or Babel? The case for official English.* Washington, DC: U.S. English.

interesting "exception":
Ramos, F. and Krashen, S. (2013). Arnold's advantages: How Governor Schwarzenegger acquired English through de facto bilingual education. *International Multilingual Research Journal* 7(3): 220–229.

native-language assessments:
Zehr, M.A. (2005, May 11). Governor Schwarzenegger vetoes changes to state exam policy. *Education Week.*

38. Why is access to print so important?
free voluntary reading:

Krashen, S. (2004). *The power of reading.* Portsmouth, NH, and Westport, CT: Heinemann and Libraries Unlimited.

reading habit transfers:
Kim, H. Y. & Cho, K.S. (2005). The influence of first language reading on second language reading and second language acquisition. *International Journal of Foreign Language Teaching* 1(4): 13–16.

rewards:
Krashen (2004).

few bookstores:
Neuman, S. & Celano, D. (2001). Access to print in low-income and middle-income communities. *Reading Research Quarterly* 36(1): 8–26.

39. How effective is bilingual education in helping children acquire or maintain their heritage language?
Language loss:
Kraus, M. (1996). Status of Native American language endangerment. In G. Cantoni (Ed.), *Stabilizing indigenous languages* (pp. 16–21). Flagstaff, AZ: Northern Arizona University.

40. What are the causes of language loss for children and communities?
language shift:
Veltman, C. (1983). *Language loss in the United States.* Berlin: Mouton.

Babel in reverse:
Haugen, E. (1972). *The ecology of languages.* Stanford, CA: Stanford University Press.

if parents speak the mother tongue:
Cho, G. & Krashen, S. (2000). The role of voluntary factors in heritage language development: How speakers can develop the heritage language on their own. *ITL: Review of Applied Linguistics* 127–128: 127–140.

41. What is ethnic ambivalence?
ethnic evasion:
Tse (2001).

42. What is language shyness?
high standards:
Krashen, S. (1998). Language shyness and heritage language development. In S. Krashen, L. Tse & J. McQuillan (Eds.), *Heritage language development* (pp. 41–49). Culver City, CA: Language Education Associates.

43. What are the criticisms of bilingual education that led to the passage of English-only initiatives in California (1998), Arizona (2000), and Massachusetts (2002)?

California:
English Language in Public Schools (1998). Proposition 227: Initiative statute.

Arizona:
English Language Education for Children in Public Schools (2000). Proposition 203: An initiative measure.

Massachusetts:
English Language Education in Public Schools (2002). Question 2: Law proposed by initiative petition.

44. ELLs score much lower on standardized tests than other students. Doesn't this show that bilingual education has failed?
faulty logic:
Crawford, J. (2008a). No Child Left Behind: Misguided approach to school accountability for English language learners. In J. Crawford (Ed.), *Advocating for English learners: Selected essays* (pp. 128–138). Clevedon, UK: Multilingual Matters.

45. Shouldn't parents have the right to choose whether their children are placed in bilingual education?
state official in California:
Crawford (2004).

46. What types of programs do the parents of ELLs favor for their children?
73% of immigrant parents:
Farkas, S., Duffet, A. & Johnson, J. (2003). *Now that I'm here: What America's immigrants have to say about life in the U.S. today.* Washington, DC: Public Agenda.

Spanish-speaking parents:
Rivera, C. (1998, Feb. 10). Bilingual classes get support in poll. *Los Angeles Times.*

Significant majorities of immigrant parents:
Shin, F. (2000). Parent attitudes toward the principles of bilingual education and their children's participation in bilingual programs. *Journal of Intercultural Studies* 21(1): 93-99.

help with homework:
Ramírez (1992).

47. Does bilingual education lead to segregation by race or ethnicity?
Hispanic students:
Orfield, G. & Lee, C. (2006). *Racial transformation and the changing nature of segregation.* Cambridge, MA: Harvard Civil Rights Project.

nearly seven in ten ELLs:
Cosentino de Cohen, C., Deterding, N., & Clewell, B.C. (2005). *Who's left behind: Immigrant children in high and low LEP schools.* Washington, DC: Urban Institute.

48. Do children "languish" in non-English classrooms for many years, never learning enough English to transfer to mainstream classrooms?
nationwide survey:
Zehler et al. (2003).

New York City:
New York City Board of Education. (2000). *Chancellor's ELL education report.* New York: Division of Assessment and Accountability.

Texas:
Texas Education Agency. (2000). *Study of possible expansion of the assessment system for limited English proficient students.* Austin, TX: Author.

California:
Parrish, T.B., Perez, M., Merickel, A. & Linquanti, R. (2006). *Effects of the implementation of Proposition 227 on the education of English learners, K–12: Findings from a five-year evaluation.* Palo Alto, CA: American Institutes for Research and WestEd.

California Department of Education. (2006). Annual language census. Online: http://dq.cde.ca.gov/dataquest/dataquest.asp.

49. Is there a tendency for schools to delay redesignating ELLs as English-proficient in states where per capita subsidies are provided to serve these children?
at least 40% more:
Dietz, J. (2004, Nov. 30). Findings of fact and conclusions of law. *West Orange Cove Consolidated ISD v. Neely.* Travis County (TX) District Court, Case No. GV-100528.

4.6 years:
Ramírez (1998).

50. What are the cost differences among various options for educating ELLs?
California study:
Chambers, J. & Parrish, T. (1992). *Meeting the challenge of diversity: An evaluation of programs for pupils with limited proficiency in English* (Vol. IV), *Cost of programs and services for LEP students.* Berkeley, CA: BW Associates.

51. How can schools teach bilingually when ELL students speak several different languages?
"unfair":
Crawford (2004).

52. Doesn't the shortage of qualified teachers make bilingual education impractical?
staff shortages:
Zehler et al. (2003).

53. If bilingual education works, why is the Hispanic dropout rate so high?
less than half:
Han, M., Baker, D. & Rodríguez, C. (1997). *A profile of policies and practices for limited English proficient students: Screening methods, program support, and teacher training.* Washington, DC: U.S. Department of Education.

18.3% of Latinos; born outside the United States:
Chapman, C., Laird, J. & KewalRamani, A. (2010). *Trends in high school dropout and completion rates in the United States: 1972–2008.* NCES 2011-012. Washington, DC: National Center for Educational Statistics.

studies suggest:
Curiel et al. (1986).

MacGregor-Mendoza, P. (1999). *Spanish and academic achievement among Midwest Mexican youth.* New York: Garland.

54. Then why do Hispanic students drop out of school at higher rates?
live with both parents:
Rumberger, R. (1991). Chicano dropouts: A review of research and policy issues. In R. Valencia (Ed.), *Chicano school failure and success* (pp. 64–89). New York: Falmer Press.

little or no difference:
Rumberger, R. (1995). Dropping out of middle school: A multilevel analysis of students and schools. *American Educational Research Journal* 32(3): 583–625.

White, M. & Kaufman, G. (1997). Language usage, social capital, and school completion among immigrants and native-born ethnic groups. *Social Science Quarterly* 78(2): 385–398.

no significant difference:
McMillen, M., Kaufman, P. & Klein, S. (1997). *Dropout rates in the United States: 1995.* NCES 97-473. Washington, DC: National Center for Educational Statistics.

high-stakes testing:
Clarke, M., Haney, W. & Madaus, G. (2000). *High stakes testing and high school completion.* Boston: National Board on Testing and Public Policy.

55. If bilingual education is such a good idea, why don't other countries provide it?

they do:
Krashen, S. (1999). *Condemned without a trial: Bogus arguments against bilingual education.* Portsmouth, NH: Heinemann.

56. Are bilingual educators promoting a hidden agenda of ethnic separatism?

La Raza Unida:
Shockley, J.S. (1974). *Chicano revolt in a Texas town.* Notre Dame, IN: Notre Dame University Press.

57. What has been the impact of English-only instruction laws?

five-year study:
Parrish et al. (2006).

Park, C.C. 2014. A retrospective look at California's implementation of Proposition 227: Focus on bilingual teacher education and student performance. In In G. McField (Ed.), *The miseducation of English learners: A tale of three states and lessons to be learned* (pp. 109–135). Charlotte, NC: Information Age Publishers.

researchers at Arizona State:
Mahoney, K., MacSwan, J. & Thompson, M. (2005). *The condition of English language learners in Arizona: 2005.* Tempe, AZ: Education Policy Studies Laboratory. Online: http://www.terpconnect.umd.edu/~macswan/EPSL-0509-110-AEPI.pdf.

Wright, W.E. & Pu, C. (2005). *Academic achievement of English language learners in post-Proposition 203 Arizona.* Tempe, AZ: Education Policy Studies Laboratory. Online: http://files.eric.ed.gov/fulltext/ED508517.pdf.

in Massachusetts:
Sacchetti, M. & Tracy, J. (2006, May 21). Bilingual law fails first test: Most students not learning English quickly. *Boston Globe.*

58. But didn't ELLs' test scores go up in California after bilingual education was eliminated?

well documented elsewhere:
Linn, R., Graue, E. & Sanders, N. (1990). Comparing state and district test results to national norms: The validity of claims that "everyone is above average." *Educational Measurement: Issues and Practice* 10: 5–14.

no differences among ELL scores:
Goto-Butler, Y., Orr, J. E., Bousquet Gutierrez, M. & Hakuta, K. (2000). Inadequate conclusions from an inadequate assessment: What can SAT-9 scores tell us about the impact of Proposition 227 in California? *Bilingual Research Journal* 24(1/2): 141–154.

Parrish, T., Linquanti, R., Merickel, A., Quick, H., Laird, J. & Esra, P. (2002). *Effects of the implementation of Proposition 227 on the education of English learners, K–12: Year 2 report.* San Francisco: WestEd.

59. What about the Oceanside school district, whose all-English programs have received so much favorable attention?

reports about student progress:
Steinberg, J. (2000, Aug. 20). Increase in test scores counters dire forecasts for bilingual ban. *New York Times.*

little or no English instruction:
Noonan, K. (2000, Sep. 3). I believed that bilingual education was best—until the kids proved me wrong. *Washington Post.*

ended abruptly:
Hakuta, K. (2003). What can we learn about the impact of Proposition 227 from SAT-9 scores? Online: http://faculty.ucmerced.edu/khakuta/research/SAT9/index.html.

Oceanside's redesignation rate:
Crawford (2004).

60. How can bilingual education be improved?

study of school libraries:
Pucci, S. (1994). Supporting Spanish-language literacy: Latino children and free reading resources in schools. *Bilingual Research Journal* 18(1/2): 67–82.

well-documented ways:
August, D. & Hakuta, K. (Eds.). (1997). *Improving schooling for language-minority children: A research agenda.* Washington, DC: National Academy Press.

Guerrero, M.D. (1997). Spanish academic language proficiency: The case of bilingual education teachers in the U.S. *Bilingual Research Journal* 21(1): 65–84.

Ramírez (1992).

61. What is constructivism and why is it beneficial for ELLs?

"something that a learner does":
Falk, B. (2009). *Teaching the way children learn* (p. 26). New York: Teachers College Press.

62. Why did the "English for the Children" initiatives pass?
73% agreed:
Los Angeles Times Poll (1998, Apr. 13). Study #410. Online:
http://diversitylearningk12.com/resources/CH13/410pa2da.pdf.

only 15%:
Crawford, J., Krashen, S. & Kim, H. (1998, Mar. 29). Anti-bilingual
initiative: Confusing in any language. Hispanic Link News Service.

2-1 margin:
Los Angeles Times Poll (1998, Jun. 2). Study #413. Online:
http://diversitylearningk12.com/resources/CH13/413pa2da.pdf.

63. What approach for educating ELLs is favored by the American public?
2003 Gallup Poll:
Hubler, E. (2003, Jul. 9). Bilingual ed backed by 58% in U.S., poll says.
Denver Post.

1998 Gallup Poll:
Gallup Poll (1999). Bilingual education. In *Public opinion, 1998.*
Wilmington, DE: Scholarly Resources, Inc.

64. What role does ethnocentrism play in public attitudes about bilingual education?
only 26%:
Huddy, L. & Sears, D. (1990). Qualified public support for bilingual
education: Some policy implications. *Annals of the American Academy of
Political and Social Science* 508: 119–134.

65. Why is the public so misinformed about bilingual programs?
remarkable disparity:
McQuillan, J. & Tse, L. (1996). Does research really matter? An analysis of
media opinion on bilingual education, 1984–1994. *Bilingual Research
Journal* 20(1): 1–27.

Crawford, J. (2008b). The bilingual education story: Why can't the news
media get it right? In J. Crawford (Ed.), *Advocating for English learners:
Selected essays* (pp. 36–50). Clevedon, UK: Multilingual Matters.

66. Does the federal government mandate bilingual education?
policy was dropped:
Jiménez, M. (1992). The educational rights of language-minority children.
In J. Crawford (Ed.), *Language loyalties: A source book on the official
English controversy* (pp. 243–251). Chicago: University of Chicago Press.

Bilingual Education Act:
P.L. 90-247 (1968, Jan. 2).

No Child Left Behind Act:
P.L. 107-110 (2002, Jan. 8).

67. Do states require schools to provide any particular instructional program for ELLs?
mandates:
Crawford (2004).

68. What are schools' legal obligations in serving ELLs?
Civil Rights Act of 1964:
42 U.S.C §§ 2000d–2000d-7 (1964).

unanimous:
Lau v. Nichols (1974). 414 U.S. 56.

San Francisco:
Crawford (2004).

69. In practice, what must school districts do to meet their obligations?
"three-prong" test:
Castañeda v. Pickard (1981). 648 F.2d 989 (5th Cir.).

Equal Educational Opportunity Act:
20 U.S.C. §1703(f) (1974).

70. Are schools responsible for educating undocumented immigrants?
1982 decision:
Plyler v. Doe (1982). 452 U.S. 202.

DREAM Act:
S. 2075 (2005). 109th Cong., 1st Sess.

71. Has the No Child Left Behind Act proved to be an effective way to "hold schools accountable" in meeting these obligations?
contradicts the spirit:
Crawford (2008a).

neither valid nor reliable:
Government Accountability Office (2006). *No Child Left Behind Act: Assistance from Education could help states better measure progress of students with limited English proficiency.* GAO-06-815. Washington, DC: Author.

72. Why not depend on "accommodations" to help ELLs cope with English-language assessments?
accommodations alone:
Abedi (2004).

73. Even if English-language achievement tests are inadequate for ELLs, what's the harm in using them?
humiliating for children:
Meyer, L.M. (2004, May 27). No Child Left Behind fails to pass fairness test. *Albuquerque Journal.*

49% in California:
California Department of Education (2003–2011). Annual language census. Online: http://dq.cde.ca.gov/dataquest/dataquest.asp.

74% in New York City:
New York City Department of Education, Office of English Language Learners. (2006). *ELLs in New York City: Student demographic data report.* New York: Author.

New York City Department of English Language Learners and Student Support. (2014). *School year 2013–2014 demographic report.* New York: Author.

74. Are you saying we should scrap testing altogether?
high-stakes decisions:
Gottlieb, M. (2003). *Large-scale assessment of English language learners.* Alexandria, VA: Teachers of English to Speakers of Other Languages.

75. If not for high stakes purposes, how should tests for ELLs be used?
improving instruction:
August & Hakuta (1997).

76. How should schools be held accountable in serving ELLs?
considering "inputs":
Crawford (2008a).

77. What makes bilingual education so politically controversial?
little or no debate:
Crawford, J. (1992). *Hold your tongue: Bilingualism and the politics of "English Only."* Reading, MA: Addison-Wesley.

78. Why do some Americans find language diversity threatening?
foreign-born population:
Gibson & Lennon (1999).

Grieco, E.M., Acosta, Y.D., de la Cruz, G.P., Gambino, C., Gryn, T., Larsen, L.J., Trevelyan, E.N. & Walters, N.P. (2012). *The foreign-born population in the United States: 2010.* Washington, DC: U.S. Census Bureau.

79. English is the official language in many countries. Why should this idea be controversial in the United States?

Turkey and Slovakia:
Kontra, M. (1999). "Don't speak Hungarian in public!": A documentation and analysis of folk linguistic rights. In M. Kontra, R. Phillipson, T. Skutnabb-Kangas & T. Várady (Eds.), *Language: A right and a resource.* Budapest: Central European University Press.

80. Isn't bilingualism a threat to national unity, dividing people along language lines?

381 different languages:
Shin, H.B. & Bruno, R. (2003). *Language use and English-speaking ability: 2000.* Washington, DC: U.S. Census Bureau.

130 nation-states:
Fishman, J.A. (1991). Interpolity perspective on the relationships between linguistic heterogeneity, civil strife, and per capita gross national product. *International Journal of Applied Linguistics* 1(1): 5–18.

81. Why has language been a source of tension in Canada?

French-speaking citizens:
Yalden, M.F. (1981). The bilingual experience in Canada. In M. Ridge (Ed.), *The new bilingualism: An American dilemma* (pp. 71–87). New Brunswick, NJ: Transaction Books.

ethnic domination:
Lemco, J. (1992). Quebec's "distinctive character" and the question of minority rights. In J. Crawford (Ed.), *Language loyalties: A source book on the official English controversy* (pp. 423–433). Chicago: University of Chicago Press.

82. When has the official language issue come up previously in U.S. history?

1923:
Baron, D. (1990). *The English-only question: An official language for Americans?* New Haven: Yale University Press.

1981:
S.J. Res. 72 (1981). 97th Cong., 1st Sess.

1996:
H.R. 123. (1996). 104th Cong., 2nd Sess.

2006:
Congressional Record. (2006, May 18). 109th Cong., 2nd Sess. (pp. S4735–4770).

83. If the United States never declared an official language in the past, didn't this reflect the fact that—until recently—most Americans spoke English and nobody demanded government services in other languages?

18 different languages:
Hansen, M.L. (1961). *The Atlantic migration, 1607–1860: A history of the continuing settlement of the United States.* New York: Harper Torchbooks.

8.6% of the population:
American Council of Learned Societies. (1931). Report of the committee on linguistic and national stocks in the population of the United States. In *Annual report of the American Historical Association.* Washington, DC: Author.

"language islands":
Hawgood, J.A. (1940). *The tragedy of German-America.* New York: Putnam.

84. What did America's founders think about the role of English?
John Adams:
Heath, S.B. (1976). A national language academy? Debate in the new nation. *International Journal of the Sociology of Language* 11: 9–43.

"make the English speak Greek":
Baron, D. (1982). *Grammar and good taste: Reforming the American language.* New Haven: Yale University Press.

85. As a practical matter, wasn't English always the language of government in America?
major colonial power:
Horwitz, T. (2006, Jul. 9). Immigration and the curse of the Black Legend. *New York Times.*

Jacques Villeré:
Crawford (1992).

translated laws:
Kloss, H. (1998). *The American bilingual tradition,* 2nd Ed. McHenry, IL: Center for Applied Linguistics and Delta Systems.

86. But isn't it true that large-scale language assistance programs such as bilingual education appeared only in the 1960s?
the first state; 600,000 children:
Kloss (1998).

87. Weren't earlier immigrants more eager to join the Melting Pot and assimilate, as compared with those arriving in recent years from Asia and Latin America?
"new immigrants":
U.S. Immigration Commission (1911). *Reports of the Immigration Commission* (Vol. 1). Washington, DC: Government Printing Office.

Deutschtum:
Hawgood (1940).

"God's Crucible":
Zangwill, I. (1909). *The melting-pot: Drama in four acts.* New York:
Macmillan. Rpt. New York: Arno Press, 1975.

"did not happen":
Glazer, N. & Moynihan, D.P. (1963). *Beyond the melting pot: The Negroes,
Puerto Ricans, Jews, Italians, and Irish of New York City.* Cambridge, MA:
MIT Press.

"Americanization" efforts:
Higham, J. (1988). *Strangers in the land: Patterns of American nativism,
1860–1925,* 2nd Ed. New Brunswick, NJ: Rutgers University Press.

**88. Are you saying that policies to restrict languages other than English are
inspired by xenophobia?**
"tough love":
Crawford, J. (2000a). Boom to bust: Official English in the 1990s. In *At war
with diversity: U.S. language policy in an age of anxiety* (pp. 31–51).
Clevedon, UK: Multilingual Matters.

barbarous dialect:
Atkins, J.D.C. (1887). Report of the Commissioner of Indian Affairs. Rpt. in
J. Crawford (Ed.), *Language loyalties: A source book on the official English
controversy* (pp. 47–51). Chicago: University of Chicago Press, 1992.

social cost:
Crawford, J. (2000b). Endangered Native American languages: What is to
be done, and why? In *At war with diversity: U.S. language policy in an age of
anxiety* (pp. 52–65). Clevedon, UK: Multilingual Matters.

89. Did European immigrant groups ever face this kind of cultural repression?
during World War I:
Luebke, F.C. (1980). Legal restrictions on foreign languages in the Great
Plains states, 1917–1923. In P. Scach (Ed.), *Languages in conflict: Linguistic
acculturation on the Great Plains.* Lincoln: University of Nebraska Press.

English-only school laws:
Leibowitz, A.H. (1969). English literacy: Legal sanction for discrimination.
Notre Dame Lawyer 45(7): 7–67.

ruled unconstitutional:
Meyer v. Nebraska (1923). 262 U.S. 390.

**90. Why does a large percentage of the public favor making English the official
language, according to opinion polls?**

already the official language:
Associated Press (1987, Feb. 14). Survey: Most Americans think English is official U.S. language.

potential impact:
Language Policy Web Site. (1997). Opinion polls on official English. Online: http://www.languagepolicy.net/archives/can-poll.htm.

forced to resign:
Crawford, J. (1988, Oct.). What's behind official English? Hispanic Link News Service. Rpt. in J. Crawford (Ed.), *Language loyalties: A source book on the official English controversy* (pp. 171–177). Chicago: University of Chicago Press, 1992.

42% of its members:
Gary C. Lawrence Co. (1988). *National telephone membership survey of U.S. English.* Santa Ana, CA: Author.

91. Immigrant languages are spreading so rapidly these days. Doesn't this trend threaten the status of English as our common language?
one in five:
Shin & Bruno (2003).

other studies:
Portes & Hao (1998); Veltman (1983).

92. How does this pattern compare with rates of English acquisition in the past?
more rapidly than ever:
Veltman (1983).

1890 census:
U.S. Census Office (1897). Can not speak English. In *Compendium of the eleventh census: 1890* (Pt. III, pp. 346–353). Washington, DC: Government Printing Office.

threatened in the United States:
Veltman, C. (2000). The American linguistic mosaic: Understanding language shift in the United States. In S.L. McKay & S.C. Wong (Eds.), *New immigrants in the United States.* Cambridge: Cambridge University Press.

93. Would it speed up English acquisition even more if government eliminated bilingual assistance programs?
1995 study:
Associated Press (1995, Sep. 27). Practically English-only.

94. Isn't it important to send a message to immigrants that they are expected to learn our language?

substantial majority; 92% say:
Pew Hispanic Center (2006). Fact sheet: Hispanic attitudes toward learning English. Washington, DC: Author. Online: http://www.pewhispanic.org/2006/06/07/hispanic-attitudes-toward-learning-english/.

waiting lists:
Pope, J. (2006, Apr. 22). Immigrants rely on patchy English teaching. *Washington Post.*

95. How do programs in other languages promote English and acculturation?
bilingual voting materials:
Washington Post (2006, Jul. 10). Yes on bilingual ballots.

96. Does this mean the United States should move toward official bilingualism, as in Canada?
systematic effort:
Executive Order 13166 (2000). Improving services for persons with limited English proficiency. Online: http://www.lep.gov/13166/eo13166.html.

97. Backers of official English have disclaimed the "English-only" label. Aren't they advocating something less extreme than that?
Voting Materials in English Only:
Crawford (1992).

"act in English":
Arizona Constitution, Art. XXVIII. (1988). English as the official language.

98. How does official English legislation violate the constitution?
struck down:
Ruíz v. Hull (1998). 191 Ariz. 441.

Meyer v. Nebraska (1923). 262 U.S. 390.

99. What is the legal impact of adopting English as the official language?
27 active official-English laws:
Language Policy Web Site (2015). Language legislation. Online: http://languagepolicy.net/archives/langleg.htm.

English Language Unity Act:
H.R. 997 (2005). 114th Cong., 1st Sess.

100. Still, isn't there something to be said for the idea of uniting Americans through a common language?
language vigilantism:
Bender, S.W. (1997). Direct democracy and distrust: The relationship between language law rhetoric and the language vigilantism experience. *Harvard Latino Law Review* 2(1): 145–174.

assault on their heritage:
Cheseborough, S. (1988, Aug. 26). McCain raps official English movement. *Phoenix Gazette.*

101. With all the ferment over language today, doesn't government need to establish a comprehensive policy?
English Plus:
H.Con.Res. 9 (2005). 109th Cong., 1st Sess.

INTERNET RESOURCES

Center for Multilingual, Multicultural Research
http://www-bcf.usc.edu/~cmmr/

James Crawford's Language Policy Web Site
http://languagepolicy.net/

DiversityLearningK12
http://diversitylearningk12.com

Institute for Language and Education Policy
http://elladvocates.org/

Stephen Krashen's Web Site
http://www.sdkrashen.com/

Modern Language Association: A Map of Languages of the United States
http://www.mla.org/map_main

National Clearinghouse for English Language Acquisition
http://www.ncela.us/

National Education Policy Center
http://nepc.colorado.edu/

University of California Linguistic Minority Research Institute
https://escholarship.org/uc/lmri

INDEX

New from The Institute for Language & Education Policy

How a Behaviorist Framework, Flawed Research, and Clever Marketing Have Come to Define – and Diminish – Sheltered Instruction for English Language Learners

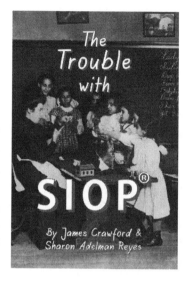

AMONG ALL THE COMMERCIAL "learning systems" on the market today, the award for most extravagant promises should go to SIOP,® the Sheltered Instruction Observation Protocol:

"Field tested ... scientifically validated ... a proven pedagogical approach [that] has helped to instruct millions of students," including not only English learners but English-proficient children, as well. There are old-time patent medicines that made fewer claims. Is SIOP a truly miraculous pedagogy — good for whatever ails you? Or is it a classic example of "research-based" hype?

The Trouble with SIOP® was inspired by a chorus of complaints from teachers required to apply the model by top-down directives. Recog-

© 2015 • 106pp • $14.95
ISBN: 978-0-9861747-0-4
Available on amazon.com
Kindle edition • $3.99
For more info:
www.elladvocates.org

nizing that SIOP had never faced much critical scrutiny, authors **James Crawford** and **Sharon Adelman Reyes** set out to determine:

Is this rigid approach, which requires teachers to incorporate "30 features and eight components" into every lesson, necessary to foster English acquisition and academic achievement? Or does SIOP, as a classic transmission model, impose a straitjacket on creative teaching and learning?

Does this heterogeneous mixture of methodologies and strategies reflect a coherent educational philosophy, consistent with research on second language acquisition? Or is SIOP essentially a grab-bag of "best practices," with a heavy emphasis on behaviorist methods?

Does research on this program support the lavish claims made on its behalf? Or is the What Works Clearinghouse at the U.S. Department of Education correct in concluding that none of the studies conducted thus far have demonstrated SIOP's effectiveness?

The answers provided by *The Trouble with SIOP*® should interest those concerned not only with the education of English language learners, but also with the pernicious impact of commercial pedagogies in American classrooms.

Also Available from
DiversityLearningK12

"A must read for parents and teachers who value bilingualism, biculturalism, and positive identity construction for their children. Highly recommended."
— *Choice*

"Refreshing and inspiring ... If you are interested in learning how educators and parents can promote language acquisition, creating inventors who think creatively and (gasp!) even achieve excellent results on academic tests, this is the book for you."
— *Creative Educator*

Diary of a
Bilingual School

❦ ❦ ❦ ❦ ❦ ❦ ❦ ❦
Sharon Adelman Reyes
& James Crawford

© 2012 • 136 pp • 6" x 9"
ISBN: 978-0-9847317-0-1
Paperback: $19.95
Kindle: $4.99
info@diversitylearningk12.com

DUAL IMMERSION, a popular new way to cultivate bilingualism, is capturing the attention of parents and educators alike. By bringing together children from diverse backgrounds to learn each other's languages in a natural setting, it has proved far more effective at cultivating fluency than traditional approaches.

But how do these programs actually work? What goes on in dual immersion classrooms? And what is it that makes them so effective?

Diary of a Bilingual School answers these questions with a unique mix of narratives and analysis. Depicting a year in the life of a 2nd grade classroom, it demonstrates what can happen when the instruction is bilingual and the curriculum is constructivist.

The book focuses on Chicago's Inter-American Magnet School, one of the nation's most acclaimed dual immersion programs, where children thrive in an environment that unlocks their intellectual curiosity and enthusiasm for learning. Simultaneously, without conscious effort, they become proficient in two languages and at home in a culture that differs from their own.

For those who want to discover the benefits of dual immersion for their children or for their students—or who want to learn more about child-centered approaches to teaching—*Diary of a Bilingual School* is a must.

ENGAGE
The Creative Arts

A Framework for
Sheltering and Scaffolding Instruction
for English Language Learners

BY
SHARON ADELMAN REYES

© 2013 • 152 pp • 8½" x 11"
$26.95
ISBN: 978-0-9847317-3-2
info@diversitylearningk12.com

Also Available from
DiversityLearningK12

"With *Engage the Creative Arts,* we are entering a new era in language instruction. This book vastly expands the options for providing second language students with what they really need: input that is both comprehensible and highly interesting, so interesting that students forget it is in another language. It is sure to make teaching second languages not only much more pleasant than current approaches, but also much more effective."

— *Stephen Krashen, Professor Emeritus University of Southern California*

MEETING THE NEEDS OF ENGLISH LANGUAGE LEARNERS is one of the biggest challenges facing American schools today. Practical classroom strategies are essential. But it is also critical for educators to understand the rationale behind them: why a technique or methodology is working or not working for their students. *Engage the Creative Arts* is designed to build that understanding while also stimulating teachers' imagination to help them invent new strategies of their own.

The book introduces the ENGAGE **Framework for Sheltering and Scaffolding Language the Natural Way.** It emphasizes methodologies that are grounded in a constructivist educational philosophy and a comprehensive theory of language acquisition. Rather than prescriptive, step-by-step recipes for instruction, it features strategies that are open-ended, creative, and best of all, engaging for students.

Engage the Creative Arts is full of hands-on, ready-to-use activities in dramatic arts, creative writing, music and rhythm, dance and movement, and visual arts, along with ideas for developing many more. But the ENGAGE Framework can be applied to any academic content area. And the strategies in this book are designed for all teachers who work with second language learners, whether in bilingual, English as a second language, dual immersion, heritage language, or world language classrooms.

Also Available from
DiversityLearningK12

LANGUAGE PROFICIENCY is multidimensional. While conversational skills are essential for social interaction, they are insufficient for most academic purposes. To be successful, teachers and students must acquire a firm and accurate command of subject-area vocabulary.

Even though a growing number of Americans speak Spanish at home, the United States has a severe shortage of professionals with fully developed academic skills in Spanish. This poses a special challenge for bilingual classrooms. Educators must be able to identify *la palabra justa* — the right word — in preparing or presenting a lesson, especially when providing content instruction and second-language input at the same time.

ENGLISH–SPANISH
ESPAÑOL–INGLÉS

La Pa-la-bra Jus-ta *f.*
the right word; correct term; appropriate vocabulary

A GLOSSARY OF
ACADEMIC VOCABULARY FOR
BILINGUAL TEACHING & LEARNING

Edited by
SHARON ADELMAN REYES
SALVADOR GABALDÓN
JOSÉ SEVERO MOREJÓN

© 2014 • 428 pp • $29.95
DiversityLearningK12 LLC
ISBN: 978-0-9847317-2-5

Recognizing an acute need, the editors of this volume brought together an international team of language teachers, teacher educators, and other bilingual professionals to create an English-Spanish/Español-Inglés glossary. *La Palabra Justa* features more than 24,000 entries covering the academic vocabulary needed in K–12 education.

Unlike a dictionary, the glossary offers a quick, user-friendly way to find translations of key terms in context. Sections include:

- **Language Arts:** *Grammar & Composition, Literature, Languages*
- **Mathematics:** *Arithmetic & Algebra, Geometry, Probability & Data Analysis, Numbers & Measures*
- **Science:** *Earth Sciences, Life Sciences, Physical Sciences, Inquiry & Process*
- **Social Studies:** *Civics & Government, Economics & Finance, Geography, History*
- **Fine Arts:** *Performing Arts, Visual Arts*
- **Technology**
- **School Life:** *Holidays & Celebrations, School Routines & Activities, Field Trips & Transportation, School Library, Playground & Sports, Student Health, Special Needs, Conduct & Discipline*

Also Available from
DiversityLearningK12

"By far the most complete, the most thorough, and the most insightful volume ever done in the field."

— Stephen Krashen
Professor Emeritus
University of Southern California

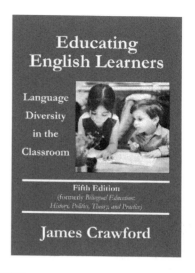

Educating English Learners

Language Diversity in the Classroom

Fifth Edition
(formerly *Bilingual Education: History, Politics, Theory, and Practice*)

James Crawford

NEWLY UPDATED
KINDLE EDITION, 2015
NOW AVAILABLE ON AMAZON

LONG POPULAR WITH STUDENTS AND PROFESSORS ALIKE, *Educating English Learners,* 5th edition (2004), differs from typical academic texts in several ways. Its journalistic style and presentation, drawn from real-world programs and events, have made it one of the most readable books used in teacher-education programs.

Author **James Crawford,** a former Washington Editor of *Education Week,* offers a broad perspective encompassing policy and politics as well as research and pedagogy. Avoiding the "everything but the kitchen sink" approach, he stresses in-depth discussions of key concepts and controversies that are most relevant to classroom teachers. Crawford relies not only on academic sources, but also on interviews he has conducted over many years with researchers, practitioners, policymakers, and advocates.

In addition, the new Kindle edition provides extensive links to bibliographical references, plus a Web-based Online Resource Guide featuring hundreds of primary source materials, research studies, legislation and litigation, ERIC Digests, historical documents, government reports, and other aids to further research.

About DiversityLearningK12

Specializing in bilingual, ESL, and multicultural education, DiversityLearningK12 is a consulting group that provides professional development, keynote presentations, program design, educational publishing, and related services. For more information, please visit us at www.diversitylearningk12.com or email us at info@diversitylearningk12.com.

Made in the USA
San Bernardino, CA
21 October 2015